Penguin Crossword Puzzles

The *Daily Telegraph*
Eighth Crossword Puzzle Book

The *Daily Telegraph* Eighth Crossword Puzzle Book

Penguin Books

PENGUIN BOOKS

Published by the Penguin Group
Penguin Books Ltd, 27 Wrights Lane, London W8 5TZ, England
Penguin Books USA Inc., 375 Hudson Street, New York, New York 10014, USA
Penguin Books Australia Ltd, Ringwood, Victoria, Australia
Penguin Books Canada Ltd, 10 Alcorn Avenue, Toronto, Ontario, Canada M4V 3B2
Penguin Books (NZ) Ltd, 182–190 Wairau Road, Auckland 10, New Zealand

Penguin Books Ltd, Registered Offices: Harmondsworth, Middlesex, England

First published in book form by Penguin Books 1961
20 19 18 17 16 15 14 13 12

Copyright © *The Daily Telegraph*, 1961
All rights reserved

Printed in England by Clays Ltd, St Ives plc
Set in Monotype Times

The Puzzles

1

1 Order an insect to be the one to take charge (10)
6 Part of a ship popular with traders (4)
9 I come between mother and her friend to some purpose (10)
10 An achievement in extremity (4)
13 Handel's is a popular oratorio
15 A prayer for direction in a zoo (6)
16 What hotels may become (6)
17 They may be good pictures without constructive effects (8, 7)
18 Opposed to a bit of poetry (6)
20 This early English archbishop gave a short reply to a tree (6)
21 It is not odd really that every day should have one (7)
22 He is four or more (4)
25 Under one kind of influence (10)
26 A part, at any rate, of 8 down (4)
27 A prominent feature of last summer (3, 7)

DOWN

1 1 across may have to look after it (4)
2 Sounds an uncertain little one (4)
3 Flighty characters? (6)
4 Is it an exaggeration to say the yeoman does it? (5, 3, 4, 3)
5 Invalid exclamation, all cut and dried (6)
7 Upset publicly at the start (10)
8 Full of spirit – and a certain amount of mineral, too? (10)
11 They are limiting factors that count in cricket matches (10)
12 To which one may retire (6, 4)
13 It is returned in code for security purposes (7)
14 Foundations there must be for a successful Government policy on this (7)
19 Indicate it may be Venice (6)
20 Articles about spirit make a complaint (8)
20 Articles about spirit make a complaint ... ps (6)
23 Some little annoyance for the scratch man ...
24 German or river in Germany (4)

ACROSS

8 Victory to one city for another (10)
9 Used some sense with material result (4)
10 What the trailer usually says about that new film! (10)
11 A chapter head (4)
12 Paris agent changes organization and arranges some pretty savage ceremonies! (5, 5)
17 A question of selection? (5)
20 Bath has close associations with it (4)
21 State of mind resulting from a reverse of fate (4)
23 Seashore features that might be nudes! (5)
24 From them may grow the makings of dreams (5, 5)
30 Hobson's choice of a letter is legally wrong (4)
31 'Mow fir belt' (anag.) (destroy his haunt? What a howling shame!) (6-4)
32 Chopping it up can give the right start to one day of the week (4)
33 The bloom of youth at its face value? (4, 6)

DOWN

1 The county that shows evidence of losing its freshness (5)
2 They are usually unwilling to swallow anything under 100 p.c. proof (8)
3 What rents may materially be (4, 2)
4 This room should be entirely safe (6)
5 A man of convictions might find it hard to get out of (6)
6 Consume after getting fed up in reverse (6)
7 Unusual feats that stupefy at first (6)
13 Should it be a crab, would the nippers pinch it? (5)
14 A disturbed dream, in preparation for war it would seem (5)
15 A bit of land that might be opened up (4)
16 Release provides it at the end, after hard labour (4)
18 One of the circles that is 19 down (4)
19 Completely consecrated (4)
22 Immerse the wild plant, but it carpets the water sti
24 Chemical remains of some burnt vessel, perha
25 Consultation after a draw to arrange replay? (6)

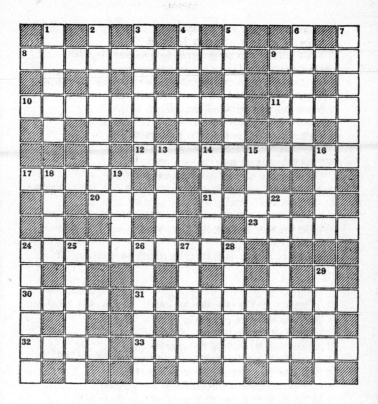

26 Ridicule is its weapon (6)
27 To do so might be the object of net play (6)
28 Parts of it are useful to writers (6)
29 Lakes may naturally be used to quench thirst (5)

ACROSS

5 Mostly one point, and the absence of it might give away three points (6)
8 Swell evidence that someone has been hooked? (5, 3)
9 Circles in bird feature as pre-nesting practice (6)
10 Circles to number and bring about in post-nesting practice (8)
11 Apparently he gave his bow to a lady (6)
12 If you don't get up before ten you may be this (7, 3)
15 Gives a big personal example when it turns to colour (5)
16 Perfectly straightforward with one's interior (6)
19 Everybody's sight screen (6)
24 Take it to gain courage (5)
27 The dainty morsel that gave a singer pang (6, 4)
28 Admitting of no rigid description (6)
29 With freedom limited and the colour in evidence (8)
30 Some gaffer you might take fishing with you in Scotland? (6)
31 What you may be doing by having business with a street corner bookmaker (8)
32 In it an M.P. finds an opening for relaxation sometimes (6)

DOWN

1 This race was once popular in the circus (7)
2 A particular relation figures in it, too (7)
3 A lion could be a this of its beginning (7)
4 A warrior to continue tediously about nothing (7)
5 A way for horses also used by coaches (3-4)
6 Card game for the senior officer on a vessel (4-3)
7 In the old army it was sticking power they showed (7)
13 It interleaves with us, in Scotland (4)
14 Mere juvenile expression of gratitude to the jolly jacks (4)
17 It's finished, so let's change sides (4)
18 Good advice to any poor beggar (4)
20 Able to avoid 5 across? (7)
21 A beater's confession produced by no steady pressure (7)
22 The right epithet for Peter Pan (7)
23 Sent aid to act as a substitute (7)

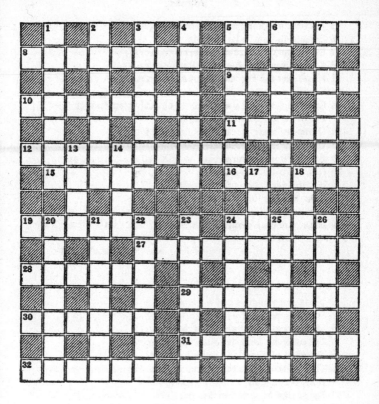

24 Receive information about the common growth (7)
25 Agrees to being dispatched with a fool outside (7)
26 TV's near giving us some stimulating places (7)

27

1 An Italian violin and full of romance (7)
8 Support an aim in late autumn (4-3)
9 It will make even cool men open an eye! (7)
10 I'm in pineapple? As well call me a liar (7)
11 How sheer the French part of a church is (7)
14 Classify a donkey a bit (6)
18 One this is probably simple but not easily seen through (5)
20 Put in the correct answer here (6)
22 Dump the vessel back, that's fine! (3-3)
23 Underground drain broken, but still able to hold water (5)
25 Famous inventor turns back to finish off the game (2, 4)
28 Its child is full of grace (7)
29 Not in dimensions difficult to fit (7)
32 A mature version of an athlete (7)
33 Food supplied in Roman road race (7)
34 Shout a narrative intrinsically true (7)

DOWN

1 It has given many a cadet the pip (10)
2 Put some nose out of joint for long periods (4)
3 Monsters not concealed in orchids here (4)
4 Turned away from that little shaver, Ted (7)
5 The chief pig-food on a sailing vessel (8)
6 There is no need to see these animals to know they're there! (6)
7 Dark presumably, and not cricket (6)
12 Please sign in part, it makes things more comfortable (5)
13 Skinned, yes – it made father flush (5)
15 If engines do it up there's no moving them (5)
16 To spread out grass under an animal in Surrey (5)
17 Famous little black girl starts this confusion (5-5)
19 One of those a dramatic Roman asked to borrow (3)
21 A handy substitute for clumsy fingers (8)
24 Little Charles and Thomas together discover little Mary! (7)
26 To do with something you are using now (6)

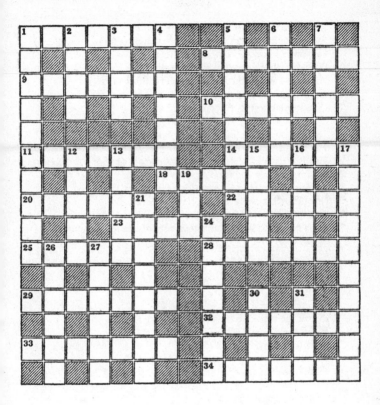

27 Good advice to drum into a batsman to keep? (6)
30 It admits one certainly but not to a high degree (4)
31 Old ruler of the Nore (4)

28

1 It's the purse money he's after! (10)

8 Every exciting romance should have this drug (6)

9 Significance arising from pact in Rome (10)

10 Edward first put back ale in high spirits (6)

11 Where in London the poor man gets confused (10)

12 The proper study of mankind must include these (6)

13 Composition to mope about (4)

15 Completely contain, yet fail for the greater part (7)

19 Tiddley concoction liable to make one feel blown up! (7)

21 The shop always displays one (4)

22 This is usually indicative of the first person (6)

25 Starts contrarily and is one way to start an argument (10)

27 An Eastern to subject a vowel to grammatical dissection (6)

28 One thing that never lets the Navy down (6, 4)

29 Plan for giving science start to another fellow and self (6)

30 In no condition to maintain constancy of bearing without stern control (10)

DOWN

1 Flowery example of rim in writing (8)

2 One of the more arresting bits of change (6)

3 Fragment in friend formed to entrance (6)

4 Hold with serpentine tail (5)

5 His progress may be a question of time (3, 5)

6 Fulfilled one of the conditions of living, perhaps (8)

7 Initial S.A. War fighting unit and the rest at presentation of zoological specimen (5-3)

13 Go both ways (3)

14 What someone may take, given less (3)

16 A shade of difference about is causing bother (8)

17 The artist who never knew what was going to happen when he went to sea? (8)

18 He was devilish clever! (8)

20 Her work, though perhaps of periodical importance might bring her to book (8)

23 It supports stable rations to eat in France (6)
24 Four rising with anger, commonly. How like a man! (6)
26 Two behind 22 across (5)

ACROSS

1 To give a Greek recitation on a feline might cause disaster (11)
7 Descriptive of certain old customs (7)
8 Naughty boy everyone comes to disparage (7)
10 Half 5 down in distress (4)
11 A manuscript written in cipher 10 (5)
13 Employer of a ruse (4)
15 Came first in the original edition (3)
17 In the borders he's on the Continent (6)
19 I ran union under another name (6)
20 A correspondence friend subject to punishment (7)
21 I have little colour when all is run through (6)
23 Cried like a dog (6)
25 It starts each week but no day (3)
27 '... makes us rather bear those —— we have than fly to others' (*Hamlet*) (4)
28 Standing order for headwear, perhaps (5)
29 A song from Mariana (4)
32 Dispel fifty upset (7)
33 Insect on the slope in heraldic terminology (7)
34 Encouraging remark by his friends to Methuselah? (5, 3, 3)

DOWN

1 Do any die from it? A hundred, for a start (7)
2 Men turn it sometimes when their hearts are weak (4)
3 In which we train for life, often changing our form (6)
4 The plunger probably gets inured to being this (6)
5 Affectionate name for Haydn (4)
6 Passes almost all small mistakes (7)
7 Would make a cup series if spread out flat (11)
9 Severe and secure like the laws of the Medes (4, 3, 4)
12 Not the way to make our money go further (7)
14 A law-maker in the drink – surely that's enough! (5)
16 Famous admiral who gave entry? (5)
18 What 16 down was able to do with himself beheaded (3)

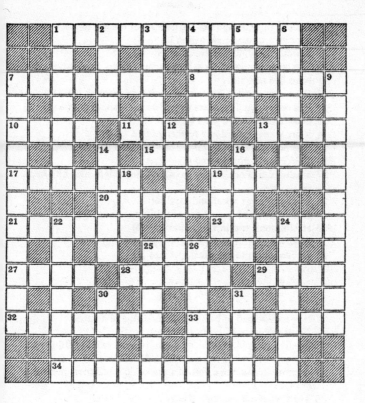

19 Fold work (3)
22 Riding thus is a double transport economy (7)
24 Have a share in (7)
25 This land on the contrary is as united as any town in England (6)
26 Fur which gives up atmosphere to fruit (6)
30 He is almost a serf (4)
31 Surrounded more than a thousand in these present days (4)

ACROSS

5 Initially this creature has the backing of the law (6)
8 Song in a transatlantic region (8)
9 Strong enough to deprive us mostly (6)
10 The exasperations of it sometimes make housewives this beheaded mad (8)
11 Often a favourite Christmas present for a bookish child (6)
12 It is seen at land frontiers as well as sea ones, of course (8)
15 Showing it in colour in a big way (5)
16 More widely spread and formerly cared for (8)
19 A strong box made by taking one nut from two trees (3, 5)
24 Husky product of Ireland (5)
27 Small holes in one's furniture should not induce such bitterness (8)
28 Source of news vocal and local (6)
29 Familiar type of animal to put spirit in an insect (8)
30 Having some end in view, obviously (6)
31 Having a central tax, but highly spoken of (8)
32 Inclines down to the edges, perhaps (6)

DOWN

1 It is accustomed to being downtrodden, and damped (4-3)
2 There are heaps of it in gardens (7)
3 It might be used to make spears to hunt the wild board (3-4)
4 A resort tending to create opening difficulties? (7)
5 Authoritative commission of irresponsible bellicose utterances (7)
6 The French veto is applied (7)
7 Puts chaos on time in place of acting (7)
13 Post for stand-to for post-mess action? (4)
14 Once you find this you will certainly be on the track (4)
17 It is actually a real place, though made up (4)
18 If you are unfortunate enough to get the bird it will not be this one (4)
20 This plant has just one spot on it inside (7)
21 What to practise at to mould oneself into a good fisherman? (7)

30

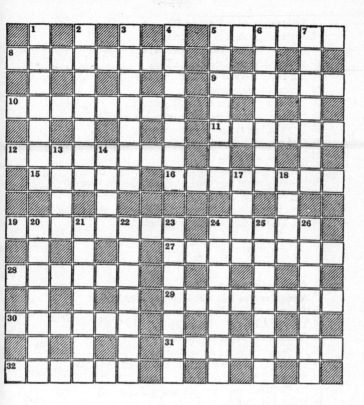

22 A fast one to put over in speech (7)
23 Persuaded into revolution by active hands (7)
24 Advance on behalf of one of the small things (7)
25 His stock will certainly this should a gardener grow less . . . (7)
26 . . . but he can never grow this (7)

31

1 End rage in explosive form (7)
8 Some of the ways of the world (7)
9 Drink in beakers like a simpleton (7)
10 Make piano and plaything talk (7)
11 It is published and very often popular (7)
14 Fruits like grain inside (6)
18 The elemental spirit of Les Sylphides (5)
20 Father gets round a deity to provide a building (6)
22 If in this one should be in control (6)
23 Dial one for a great story (5)
25 Order as prescribed (6)
28 One part of Rousseau is quite burdensome (7)
29 '—— are frogs, they drink and talk' (George Herbert) (7)
32 A gentle word, this (7)
33 Since it's about the French the result will be no rumpus (7)
34 Craft that is used in many a kitchen (7)

DOWN

1 A spirited zoo man? (10)
2 A poacher may deal with these potential birds (4)
3 This is in the middle of a dim rising (4)
4 The standards of former officers (7)
5 Covers and extends beyond (8)
6 At the beginning as a reference (6)
7 His Magic Circle was perhaps the Round Table (6)
12 A mass of metal used in melting others (5)
13 I'd climb in a roundabout country like this (5)
15 Here's the rub! (5)
16 Set entertainment no doubt, but this activity may be highly dangerous (5)
17 Pets' rest is her disturbance (10)
19 Is this archaic? Yes, it is (3)
21 The pepper that is finally frozen (8)
24 SS bends (7)
26 99 on 99 is all to do with images (6)

27 There's a rule somehow that includes a saint in Ireland (6)
30 This room is not the chief one of course (4)
31 To be legal this follows Lent, for instance (4)

32

ACROSS

5 Strong enough to deprive us mostly (6)

8 A mode of life it's idle to pursue (8)

9 Many out of practice, and not in good temper (6)

10 Safe terms of a deal, if one has a disguised cad to be harsh about (4, 4)

11 Those whose views are clearly defined may have no use for him (8)

12 If it's a spot in England, it is in Kent possibly (4)

14 Do some negative work (3)

15 A key man under the Home Secretary (6)

16 Mix paste with skill to accomplish isolation (3, 5)

19 ' "Come in!" —— —— cried, looking bigger' (Browning) (3, 5)

23 Home to such a one might be a real institution (6)

26 To sing about it is doing no good (3)

27 A fast time not confined to one race (4)

28 Suitable spell for photographing winter sports (4, 4)

29 Counsel in action, softly ahead (8)

31 A long-haired specimen, with a cap back to front (6)

32 He's not of the commoner sort (8)

33 Warm endings to certain months (6)

DOWN

1 A disease that ends in song (7)

2 Given, perhaps, but not with any good grace (7)

3 One of those women coppers? (4)

4 They have a habit of strongly pressing the unwilling to dinner! (7)

5 Part of the show? Ah, that's telling! (10)

6 Bird prized in university sport (4-3)

7 Suitable weather for putting up tents and roundabouts (3, 4)

12 Turn marbles to slap in America (4)

13 To be trusted, though mostly to be sorry for (4)

14 Bar sayings contributed by this loud-mouthed fool (7, 3)

17 The end of a moustache (4)

18 Strike it and decamp (4)

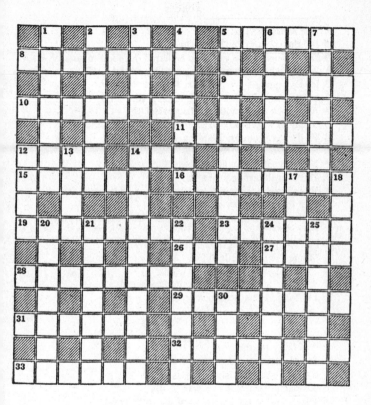

20 American version of the hooligan (7)
21 Turn to help within the boundary, and play peacemaker (7)
22 Destructive action that could lead to tears (7)
24 Not a swift worker, not even at heart (7)
25 His sayings were not 13 down (7)
30 One of the great rivers of Europe (4)

33

ACROSS

1 One surely can't be in it for pleasure? (8)
5 Fill the gap and don't retire (4, 2)
9 No! Selima would not have preferred this food to goldfish (8)
11 Seems a change from opening a door with a key (6)
12 It may convey a catchy device (4)
13 Many a skilful man has gone to table with it (3)
14 A set-back to a graduate becomes less (6)
15 It may be a sore blow to the loser not to get this prize (4-4)
18 To do so may mean following a dotty line! (4)
20 A knock-out drink, maybe (5)
21 Number noticed about tea-time (5)
22 This elf will certainly be a she (4)
24 Transferred temporarily (and has been once before?) (8)
28 Toss to and fro very quietly in an East European (6)
29 If cook said it just slipped from her hands she was probably right (3)
30 State of mind that is sometimes imperative (4)
32 Manage to make little difference to a famous composer (6)
34 They find rents, and often do repairs (8)
35 A row with the civil engineer in sequence (6)
36 Husband in red, freshened up (8)

DOWN

1 It's dry in a bit and cut in two (6)
2 Spring first, it should warm you up (6)
3 As much as a lesson in a way (2, 4)
4 Dispatched at the beginning of the sentence (4)
6 The beginning of 35 across (3)
7 Growth the Scots own is a tropical production (8)
8 An urgent matter of iron application (8)
10 'Ongar' (anag.) (where gas is manufactured?) (5)
11 Pens leap in Ireland to reform this rascal (8)
16 It's the same composition without us as with (4)
17 I crave pardon to dissent (6, 2)
18 The dry part of these reports (4)

19 A method of approach confined to golfers (4-4)
20 Malice with this is deliberate (8)
23 It is nothing in a northerner to dart off (5)
25 Hence! (6)
26 He may well be embarrassed, owing to someone or other (6)
27 Applies to one who hasn't managed to save his skin (6)
31 Dry tract for a sound churchman (4)
33 Continental water, of considerable value in India (3)

34

1 First act to start the play (4-3)

5 Their hands no doubt vary, but they are bone hearted (7)

9 Award for a man of disarming persuasiveness? (5, 5, 5)

10 Slight example of a depressed area (4)

11 Part of a ship the captain has to live on so to speak (5)

12 A dandy about middle age has not made a success of things (4)

15 Marked by shady spots (7)

16 Vegetable produce of a rough lake beside the sea (3-4)

17 Ask him about Burma, and make a note about part of India (7)

19 There's a fair chance of finding buried treasure here (4-3)

21 An untrustworthy person turns to the bar (4)

22 Capital equality is (5)

23 Hers was an exalted position, by Jove! (4)

26 'Settle cult in lea' (anag.) (to suit some highbrow circle) (12, 3)

27 The retiring sort don't stay in it (7)

28 There's nothing in the list to make one cocky! (7)

1 United it stands for our own (7)

2 'I bet I can stir men' (anag.) (assertion from the Front Bench perhaps) (7, 8)

3 When seas are this sea birds suffer (4)

4 Financially crippled owing to someone's wool-gathering? (7)

5 They shoot up, like certain fish (7)

6 The line to take, when stranded (4)

7 Flaming omen that may please the shepherd? (9, 6)

8 Jack went up it (but not Jill) (7)

13 Boy to be around for a sharp example (5)

14 Very ordinary, with forbidding start (5)

17 Cream of the West Country might be so described (7)

18 Tantalizing puzzles of some sort (7)

19 For safety treat this injury as this beheaded would have advised (7)

20 Fishy example of fifty in a straw (7)

24 The opposite of a dirge? (4)

25 A long way above zero, so a warm game no doubt (4)

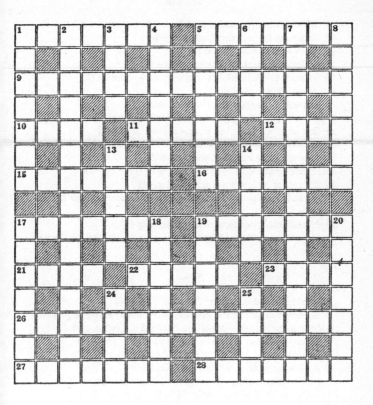

ACROSS

1 Between wise men and a friend tries, in a way, like a J.P. (13)
10 Reception for a champion layer? (7)
11 Every single elector has it (3, 4)
12 A welcome snack to a hungry fisherman (4)
13 Superior connexions, has this lake in N. America (5)
14 Draws round necks (4)
17 Exit ape to pay for its monkey tricks! (7)
18 It forms part of many a broken English strand (7)
19 One of many needed to put up a good show? (7)
22 A defence against 30 across (7)
24 Toboggan one has mostly to pull (4)
25 He may make sails in the States (5)
26 His rendering is not always popular! (4)
29 Do little details fall through where this radio linkage is concerned? (7)
30 Painful result, perhaps, of a real tanning (7)
31 The old team, Sir, will manage to look after you in Continental style (7, 6)

DOWN

2 Is this checked or waiting for a bus? (2, 1, 4)
3 The town of St Francis has this river running up through it (4)
4 May mean hair off but with its head off it'd be on, sure (7)
5 Disorderly place in S. America to us (7)
6 In the middle of the morning, he's audibly hesitant (4)
7 Appearing to be a card game expert (7)
8 Only possible surely by an ambidextrous card-sharper (6-7)
9 Decides not to meddle with the water supply (4, 4, 5)
15 Many are swallowed by degrees, so it's obviously dangerous (5)
16 One dropped in shallow water finds it deep and foreign (5)
20 Mountainous meal, maybe (4, 3)
21 It has been known to become a torrent (7)
22 Quietly lifted to be commended above one's fellows (7)
23 An illness that takes a strong hold? (7)
27 The sort of job that is often a put-up one? (4)
28 Two prepositions not one provides it (4)

36

1 Hardly food for thought, but it's often retailed for popular consumption (4, 3, 5)
8 She might seem to offer considerable refreshment (7)
9 Certainly applicable to the passage of time (3-4)
11 I owe you runs? That might be devastating (7)
12 Call in something to pacify, from the sea (7)
13 One of the bars that provide stingo (5)
14 What the ill-fated Queen of the May requested (5, 4)
16 Clean muddle in poet, like an unclean hull (9)
19 Even an illiterate could figure how to read it ... (5)
21 ... by observation of this kind (7)
23 A study of it aids one to get some calculating expression into letters (7)
24 Defensive example of marine creature about to back the law (3-4)
25 Hot rice mixture anciently pertaining to public spectacles (7)
26 Trees to Dutch appear to be extended (9, 3)

1 The bunch of blue ribbon Johnny promised to bring, for example (7)
2 It might be quite feasible to bottle it up behind the bar (7)
3 They were reassuring watch-words (3, 2, 4)
4 Warnings of things to avoid? (5)
5 They love their Soccer here, though suspended at first (7)
6 Congratulate the girl on your knee! (7)
7 Road features providing an arch in lock fastenings (7, 5)
10 What a democratic poll is meant to discover? (7, 5)
15 An East European herd, perhaps (3, 6)
17 When men are at sixes and sevens in empty words this is what remains (7)
18 Area of the disordered race in time (7)
19 Game not calculated to produce sparks (7)
20 Covering for chairs, with sober edging to a bare main part (7)
22 This brings no comfort to the middle man (5)

37

ACROSS

7 ——— ——— ——— (*Hamlet*) (6, 2, 7)
8 A ship may run it with disastrous results (7)
10 Naturally they are ultra-violet (3-4)
11 Black heraldic creature (5)
12 What the lotus-eater does (5)
14 Everyone is almost in debt you must admit (5)
15 These creatures make a celestial come-back (4)
16 Cots might have this down in part of England (4)
17 Level that in poetry often lacks number (4)
19 A warmer for most of a nursery Miss (4)
21 Active return of 51 in time (5)
22 Try to get round the gunners going back to stay here (5)
23 To reckon up is noble (5)
25 A very deep voice has nothing on this orchestral piece (7)
26 An old explorer returns with some company and goes up in smoke (7)
27 'It trains a mind so' (anag.) (15)

DOWN

1 A uniformed band of railway officials? (7, 2, 6)
2 A game of many colours played on the green (7)
3 These overalls may well be hers (5)
4 Entertainment to be seen more than once? (5)
5 This size of type is a gem of a colour (7)
6 A sport that has its traps and involves many a gamble (9-6)
9 A platform for what might be said (4)
10 Go it! That's not hard work! (4)
13 Soothe with another form of waltz (5)
14 A room high up (5)
17 Being flexible I get into the castle ruins (7)
18 Circles in similar directions for a time (4)
19 It grows and makes a lot of money (4)
20 Can't if a too keen person emerges (7)
23 Funny bit of commentary on a couple of Roman figures (5)
24 Yesterday's tomorrow (5)

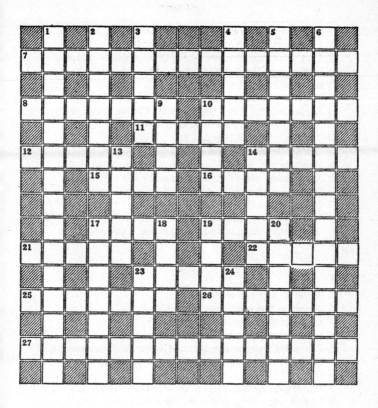

38

ACROSS

1 Strand may be the site of this temporary building (4-6)
9 Caution will lead to conflict if curtailed (4)
10 They don't trample on the bed of the Channel, of course! (5, 5)
11 It takes more than a slight jerk to uproot this grass (6)
12 Extract considered not wise in Paris (7)
15 It sounds in even time (7)
16 The animal that shows great vivacity if its tail is cut off (5)
17 It encourages lying, one must admit (4)
18 Finished feature of 10 across (4)
19 One hardly worthy of his hire (5)
21 Was once in a ferment, but idle now as constituted (3, 4)
22 A convenient place from which to give one's address (7)
24 Steps to be taken preliminary to a landing? (6)
27 One of a series that is to be continued (10)
28 Fuel to feed the furnace, and all right in the civil engineer (4)
29 'Hid relapse' (anag.) (good work by some high-up?) (10)

DOWN

2 Showing great expectation (4)
3 Visions of lots and lots of paper (6)
4 Soften us up as time comes around (7)
5 Cultivate what may provide some change (4)
6 Part of the metropolis which church-goers must face up to (4, 3)
7 Device used by architects skilful about suggestion of opposition (10)
8 Where good packing helps towards possession (2, 3, 5)
12 Licensees may often be seen leaving it (4, 6)
13 One does not need a hard head to take them (4, 6)
14 Omit with central cover (5)
15 This used to hold a good quantity of 21 across (5)
19 Give a brief sign of endorsement (7)
20 Boy with a waster around makes sound runs (7)
23 Owner of two famous London banks (6)
25 An extensive land area, as I admit in part (4)
26 In at the making of a contrary suggestion (4)

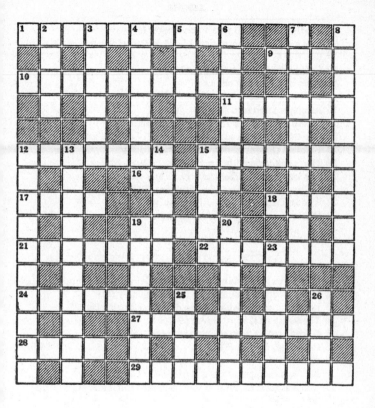

ACROSS

8 Equality a spot will give a non-worker (8)
9 This kind of demonstration should not require much explanation (6)
10 Endowed with rhythmical feet? (8)
12 A set-back about a colour (6)
14 He doesn't believe in the outdoor life? (4-2-4)
18 Its hall is famous in song (4)
21 A case which is this requires sharp attention (2, 5)
22 One military corps seems unconvinced of this defence (7)
23 Finished all square, not loosely speaking (4)
25 Mac's gait it might be (can't he see?) (10)
28 The lazy ones go after the doctor (6)
30 I'm at the heart of a Roman orator, all metal (8)
32 A most fitting occupation to follow (6)
33 Half a distorted story, told maybe by a pupil here (8)

DOWN

1 May be merely a classic greeting in a feline but look out! (6)
2 Justly describes a number in being imaginary (6)
3 Its revolutions provide a good deal of entertainment (4)
4 The floury ends of 10 across (4)
5 Was it used as currency in stock sales? (6)
6 Delectable flat-fish (6)
7 Appropriately a low part of the leg (4)
11 A classic example of faithful friendship (7)
13 You can get it returned in foreign money and it makes you mad (7)
14 The kind of aunt to call upon suddenly! (7)
15 It both fell and caused a fall (5)
16 Only two began it but a larger number is in it (4)
17 To be found in a tram, maybe, but out of this world! (7)
19 A bit of a lad ultimately grown up (5)
20 Orlando's old retainer, first in the race (4)
24 It may provide fuel for itself beheaded (6)
25 Join up as doubtless make certain of it (6)

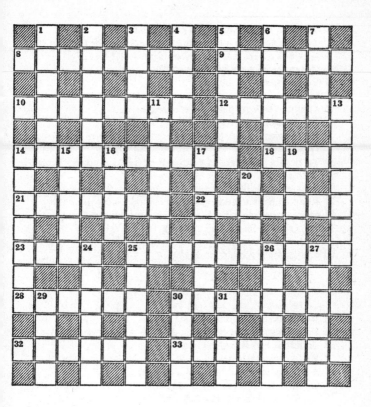

26 A margin of security may be obtained from doing so (6)
27 Take no notice (6)
29 Not a fictional coin (4)
30 As well find it in all choral societies (4)
31 Father, let me take it up first (4)

40

ACROSS

1 Turned up in cold region, in great favour (7)
5 Break this bank and dissipate liquid assets, maybe (4)
9 Folk everywhere, but no persons in particular (6, 2, 7)
10 If I go she becomes unbalanced (4)
11 Desire eagerly (5)
12 He was notable in Cathay and in Peru (4)
15 Creatures to bang hard in a reverse (7)
16 Act to produce plenty of splits in a suit (7)
17 Not keeping up with the job of preparing to prevent a freeze-up (7)
19 To explain its descent one would need, perhaps, to use a cross reference (7)
21 It sounds dove-like, but abroad is often an aggressive stroke (4)
22 Result of lighter strike puts many in public recognition (5)
23 One may associate it with waves of unnatural consequences (4)
26 Father to the fearful man? (10, 5)
27 Back yard transport (4)
28 Epithet for tough old runners? (7)

DOWN

1 It was afternoon in the R.C.S. (3, 4)
2 One who should quickly profit from the master mind (9, 5)
3 To take it easy is nothing in the fifties (4)
4 Has a common sense ending, but is fraught with disaster (7)
5 Anything but straightforward advice (7)
6 Kinds of 15 across mostly related (4)
7 Spoil a suggestion of medicine time (7)
8 Artificial locks that can make a big difference (14)
13 '—— casements, opening on the foam of perilous seas' (Keats) (5)
14 Was fired, and bears the brunt in a way (5)
17 Every bit a match for the devil (7)
18 To which the darling of the gods may confidently look for applause (7)
19 Limbs of government, perhaps (7)

84

20 One of the quarter finals (4, 3)
24 Grossly overcook a fish? (4)
25 Sign of injury that is associated with a borough up north (4)

41

4 Bald men can't justly complain of having it (8)
8 Man-invented scourge which often wiped out families (8)
9 Such things are not customarily free (8)
10 Part of the Indian sub-continent (6)
11 Imploring, behold a feature to implore about (10)
16 A man fit, it seems, to be murdered (4)
18 Heart of heart but little changed (3)
19 One mist may suffice to dampen (7)
21 Balance knows no degree (5)
22 A comprehensive phrase but lacking energy (3, 2)
23 Fine metal to begin the job (5, 2)
26 Distinctive doctrine is followed by a number (3)
28 A North American lake (4)
29 Hard tasks are not usually done in them by sedentary workers (4, 6)
33 Embody characteristics of a kind (6)
35 Replace someone temporarily (8)
36 In the matter of smartness, Fawley might be a clue (8)
37 Loud and torn garment, or a bit of it (8)

1 A bill that is presented before any order is complied with (4)
2 They provide curious work for the handyman (3, 4)
3 Bulb set in a harvested cornfield (7)
4 Father thus looking up around the walls (5)
5 Trap her beneath it all (6)
6 Get to a bit of the river (5)
7 Look in the marsh for the rogue (5)
10 Diffusive advice that begins through self (8)
12 This Court is maintained daily in West London (5)
13 Its contents might be liquid or mineral (6)
14 Neat in make-up and natural in character (6)
15 This island is continually being worn out (8)
16 Passages as holding 15 down, for example (6)
17 Direction in moral setting of races (6)

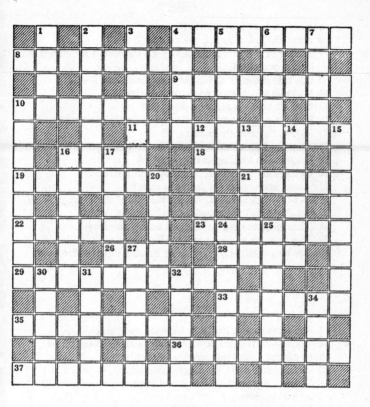

20 She is fifty short of being usual (5)
24 Part of a Test if yet to be played (7)
25 Boys' verdict which may make them burst into tears? (7)
27 An object of reverence to many (6)
30 18 across joins me in creating a ruler (5)
31 Immature author? (5)
32 Nitre is one source of it (5)
34 A distant number in the country (4)

ACROSS

1 A successor of Mohammed (6)
4 A striking bid, though a modest one (4)
7 To talk of a boxer being this by his opponent's haymakers is fistic hyperbole (4, 4)
8 One may strive for it, but the cause must come first (6)
10 Might be said of trees given spray treatment (8)
13 Wine on board produces violent effects (6)
14 Brook in a settlement in India represented in African fauna (7)
15 To do so is certainly revealing (6)
18 Bid a run be used to free locks (7)
19 Headless fish blotting its copy book (6)
20 Its high calling is not unconnected with 1 across (7)
25 Samuel has a vessel for Eastern waters (6)
26 To be put out of countenance in the land of the 25 across (4, 4)
27 Metal with soft wrapping common in the navy (6)
28 It has long standing associations on the railways (8)
29 They have got many a perch, oddly enough (4)
30 A rowing coach may get it, as he includes those he directs (6)

DOWN

1 Fish takes in war, but he won't stand and fight! (6)
2 While doing it at the docks are they slack about noise? (6)
3 Munition of war that made the captured soldier turn colour (6)
5 It can pursue a straight course in the ring (4, 4)
6 Garment that, without the second letter, includes trunks (8)
7 A sham to crush (4)
9 It lets us come to a struggle (6)
11 For the cricketer this means walking out, really (5, 2)
12 Of regular occurrence, keeping vessel in face (7)
13 Instruments of current regulation (7)
16 A destructive operator sometimes on lines of communication (6)
17 His efforts may provide one with good company (8)
18 Like a crewless ship or 1 down (8)
21 The effect of this style in building was never very plain (6)

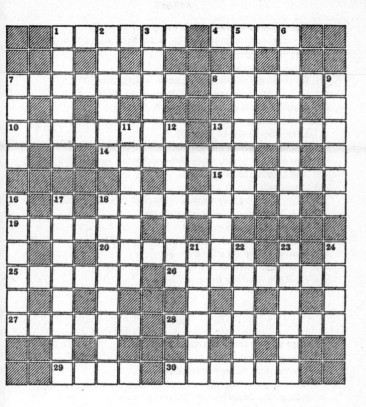

22 An incentive to flying (6)
23 One of those wicked wax-works (6)
24 When this is small it smacks of trifling things (4)

43

1 Observe present and past move up and down (6)
5 A non-drinker surrounded by drink becomes quite a gambler (6)
10 A hill and landing-place in Devon (7)
11 When people suffer from it, much is forgotten (7)
12 Study with some fervour and take counsel (6)
15 A suitable promenade for shop walkers? (6)
16 Registers that automatically go round and round (7)
17 Dress item in the window (4)
18 A coin of Central Europe (4)
19 Compacts in which many clubs endeavour to take the lead (7)
20 Mimic eats a letter in church (4)
22 Direction's able to look (4)
25 Hired somehow to go round an ancient city, and quickly! (7)
27 This Scots spirit is well watered! (6)
28 Visions of sappers in blocks (6)
31 Originate a backward name and eat badly (7)
32 It may depend on a little girl (7)
33 Grand one perhaps, the vessel over there (6)
34 Doodle's associate in America (6)

DOWN

2 Slips up and goes in to make journeys (7)
3 A vessel that is sometimes reported to be airborne (6)
4 Companions of means, often (4)
5 You need another form of garb for this game (4)
6 Voices that begin with a definite number (6)
7 Catch this (7)
8 These flowers were once used for punishment (6)
9 The gift of an ancient coin (6)
13 Entertainment about the French in providing income (7)
14 One who commits it might be said to be guilty of a form of flattery (7)
15 Beset by possible dread he stuck to it all (7)
20 A joint ornament (6)

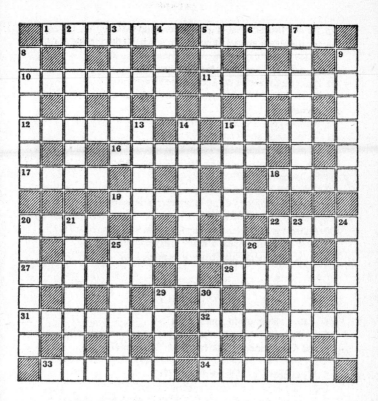

21 Edible consort (7)
23 To play it one must put on a wordy act (7)
24 Sent crazy at first, but all settle comfortably (6)
25 A legal term: amusement is devoid of it (6)
26 This monster is descriptive of a certain fly (6)
29 A sea-bird of the Western Isles (4)
30 A word to suit the active (4)

44

5 He can foretell what is going to crop up (6)

8 Send out one animal in return for a coastal description (8)

9 Mac's a useful companion when this is over (6)

10 A pretty climber ends up with a song (8)

11 Assort into certain cooked things (6)

12 The kind of stage performer to look carefully around the agencies (8)

15 Roman gods are centred in cash (6)

16 Alone it can show its royal origin (8)

19 Diana dismembered and tinned, produce of the Commonwealth (8)

24 Nails scattered with fatal result (5)

27 Epithet for the sort of thing no one cares for (8)

28 Confession of long delay in representations (6)

29 Many trying to catch fish are using the dry squeeze method (8)

30 A Dickens character who might have made things hum? (6)

31 Rose and geum make a really grisly combination (8)

32 Ruler who could turn nasty if beheaded (6)

DOWN

1 A Roman temple in America (7)

2 He shows a foreign version of what he sells torn up (7)

3 Old foreign money sounds like swift waters (7)

4 A clever man in guiding strings stays (7)

5 A sad occasion of grave finality (7)

6 Bit of butter as a barrier against danger? (7)

7 It has no use for degrees, they are not at all in its line (7)

13 The chief part of 4 down (4)

14 Latin is such a language (4)

17 Lies, perhaps, in liquid setting (4)

18 Unproductive and a bit of a riddle (4)

20 You will find many barrels in it, no doubt (7)

21 Using this those who write letters expect to get answers (7)

22 The fellow to do it is an examiner, of course (7)

23 Spicy example of precious stone turning up in seeds (7)

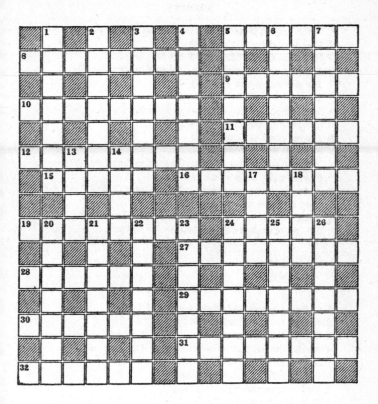

24 One rises to it and puts up outside (5, 2)
25 One can hardly do it scientifically without knowing the elements of chemistry (7)
26 A wedding gift from groom to bride (3, 4)

45

ACROSS

1 In the main a fabulous bird of material significance (8)
5 This door should be kept locked! (6)
9 Historical contrast to Light Years? (4, 4)
10 A form of oil-tax which may find itself in the soup (6)
12 The girl with a nice heart (9)
13 Wine for me and some doctor (5)
14 Sole companion that one may turn on (4)
16 Handyman who starts with skill (7)
19 The old curse of Osmanli (7)
21 Fifty less than 3 down (4)
24 If set the wrong way, these stalks produce blemishes (5)
25 Clothes easily adapted for garden use (9)
27 At 14 across, no smart way to follow down (2, 4)
28 They act quite thoughtlessly (8)
29 What we have all done at the break of a new day (6)
30 The girl who shows discretion (8)

DOWN

1 I take 13 across and attend a patient (6)
2 A most unusual thing to come across (6)
3 Cambridge College (5)
4 A cold rise but fine for tobogganing (3-4)
6 It reveals the cost of travel of a kind (9)
7 Flatter with a smooth opening (8)
8 Embracing tightly (8)
11 Plenary without peer (4)
15 The Spanish sew in this place but in a different position (9)
17 He is sent on some unpleasant errand, usually (8)
18 Only E. C. Bentley can define this rhyme (8)
20 This will give you only a bare idea (4)
21 What the schoolboy hopes his horse-chestnut will do? (7)
22 Marshal some favourite before the Scots own (6)
23 Many a P.O.W. hoped to achieve it by underground methods (6)
26 Audibly granted leave? (5)

45

95

46

1 It finds arrivals more wearing than departures (7)
5 It could be a scratch affair to those on it beheaded (7)
9 A mean line to take (even though it may be white) (6, 2, 3, 4)
10 Shakespeare says it oft loses both itself and friend (4)
11 It is really charming to find children do it correctly (5)
12 It sounds calculating and is pretty sharp (4)
15 It is through his pupils that enlightened knowledge mostly comes (7)
16 Seaside rope-makers (7)
17 Though corrosive it serves to ensure that the colours stand fast (7)
19 Arms are exercised in this before the line is occupied (4-3)
21 Sh! Love twice arranged a rendezvous for a meal in London (4)
22 Colloquially not calm in mind (5)
23 It isn't very often they are hot and cross (4)
26 What everybody knows (6, 9)
27 Village cobbler goes in ninth wicket down? (4, 3)
28 Semi-strike in part of the ship is given the bird (7)

1 Not everybody has the cheek to exhibit them (7)
2 Affectionate name for a famous runner with a capital finish (3, 6, 6)
3 Spot a little digger (4)
4 The soldier who shows a poor return in part (7)
5 Once they have yielded up 6 down they are dead men ... (7)
6 ... and sale is out of order (4)
7 Contents of those dreadful books boys love to read! (5, 3, 7)
8 A good round description? (7)
13 Cover for many at the top of the tree (5)
14 Effrontery that is not unalloyed (5)
17 I sum up first, and the verdict is euphonious (7)
18 Action to take when an increase in density is desirable (7)
19 The key to this may hang on a ring (7)

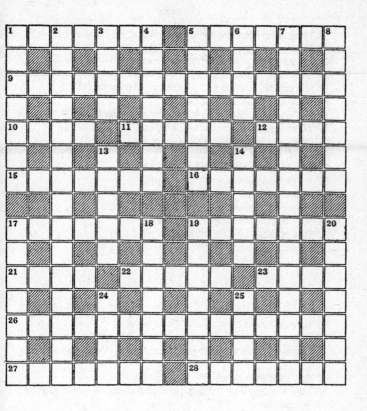

20 Famous writer who finished up as rather a dandy (7)
24 One of the big noises popular in trade (4)
25 Not one of those happy expressions (4)

ACROSS

8 There is no nonsense about him and nothing imaginary (1, 4, 3)

9 A written reference to last month (6)

10 He may have just left school or be an 8 across (3. 3)

11 One who has a consuming interest in his fellows (8)

12 He includes listeners and may make sad progress (6)

13 Individual powers in exercise (8)

15 A Yorkshire one may be broad – many are, certainly (4)

17 There is panic in the Roman fish-pond (7)

19 Often a good guide to a good judge (7)

22 Dead, but not dead on time (4)

24 In spite of everything (5, 3)

27 An Olympic winter event (6)

29 Vulgar publicity (8)

30 Rugby term of sartorial importance (6)

31 May be L is one to give injury (6)

32 One of those who see most of the game (8)

DOWN

1 A young salmon (6)

2 Epithet for the behaviour of 11 across (8)

3 Many peer into this if they look high enough (8)

4 It may provide a sound preliminary to an opening movement (7)

5 One of Shakespeare's fruity boors (6)

6 Has binding and leading possibilities and may be soundly scraped (6)

7 I have 2000 about once and inherent (8)

14 A base for young fliers in training? (4)

16 Visit a number overall (4)

18 This kind of ray may be used in photography but is rare internally (5-3)

20 It often takes this to establish a point in a 19 across (4, 4)

21 They may be on the track but out of the picture (8)

23 A matter of some gravity to those who like things neat (7)

25 It could be a miracle to find a thousand with this cake (6)
26 The painful part of the teaching profession (6)
28 Fruit in animal shape (6)

48

1 A hearty sounding quick-step? (3-1-3)
5 What the poor horse set eyes on had sharper teeth than his (4-3)
9 An affair in which a man plays the central part, naturally (7)
10 Document that carries little weight around part of W. Scotland (7)
11 These have been occasions for increments for ages (9)
12 One of the airy-fairy sort (5)
13 One may have this on to begin (5)
15 When this gets going it's a case of blade cut blade (4-5)
17 In a type of aircraft a cross indicates something one has to pay (6-3)
19 A little science upsets the Air Force but may be warming (5)
22 Material backing on the past President (5)
23 Unable to breathe, apparently, but there's a doctor there, luckily (9)
25 If this is around, then maybe you're in clover (7)
26 Bring me to give more strength, and fly to arms (7)
27 An anonymous deputy, who may nevertheless often figure in the limelight! (5-2)
28 It kills keenness, yet it's a change all the same (7)

1 Pointed relation of the putting up of an obstacle in a fence (7)
2 No wild sailor turns up, but quite a pet! (4, 3)
3 If this is the party spirit you may count me out (5)
4 Ides after 12 across should suggest such entertainment (3, 6)
5 They stoop to conquer (5)
6 This and 11 across are present time fixtures (9)
7 A pig, unlike this, cannot fly, but it can this beheaded (7)
8 Eye-witness version of a cockney greeting? (7)
14 A very old way to give a straight answer (5, 4)
16 They wear fine clothes unmoved, but if too hot they run (3, 6)
17 Added force could give it in time, but time's up for it (7)
18 A giant of the ring, but the carnage suggested did not occur (7)

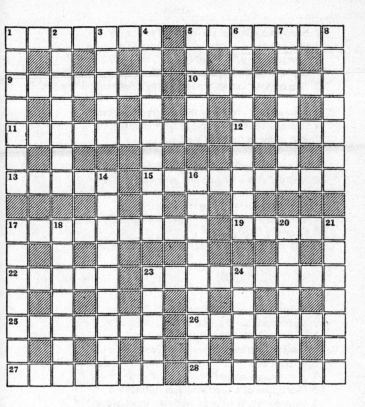

20 Certainly a place to fly from (3, 4)
21 Always on the move, but I'd get into it (7)
23 Its distinction may be social or artistic (5)
24 No doubt some women wear it because they are used to doing so (5)

49

1 Back young Samuel up with wild results (5)
4 Gnals (4-5)
9 Vegetable cut after equality (7)
11 Grave as producing destructive effects (7)
12 This crop was not grown long though it was at one time popular (4)
13 A blemish of a military force in transgression (5)
14 Combine in which everyone takes part (4)
17 Red is one in the artist's scheme (7, 6)
19 If you can claim them you are less likely to be overlooked (7, 6)
21 An arrangement of bars to which a singer is often confined (4)
22 Nothing with a blemish will get an award (5)
23 A sweet smelling cotton centre (4)
26 So ends a song of Kingston, perhaps (7)
27 Therein by arrangement both are rejected (7)
28 Grows in folds (9)
29 Fish is returned to me but it is wine that is needed (5)

1 A castor with pungent contents (6-3)
2 He had original thoughts on the subject of W/T (7)
3 Decline to put dishes in (4)
5 It may in fact have a running buffet too (8, 5)
6 It might be a perfect vase except that it's broken here (4)
7 A rotund antonym (7)
8 Descriptive of a natural violent rush (5)
10 Unimportant meetings? Not even quarter ones! (5, 8)
15 Mockery is archaic stuff (5)
16 A witty saying if creating a dominant idea artistically (5)
18 See equivalent (9)
19 As good as old English gold? (7)
20 Did some cracking of shells, perhaps (7)
21 Plants of volcanic activity (5)
24 A painter of little work, that is obvious (4)
25 Is its trade not liable to fluctuations? (4)

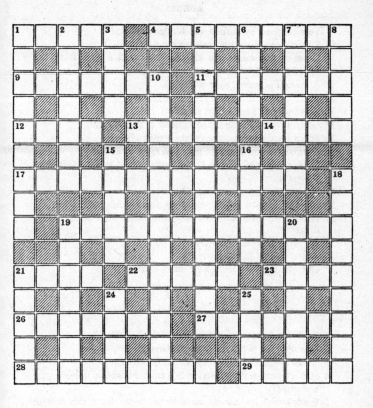

50

1 Version given by airman and foreign notable (7)
5 This is hunted not for perfume but for fur (4-3)
9 Cavalier treatment was all that he could expect from the opposition (15)
10 A foreign prince of sour quality (4)
11 When down-trodden it may be the cause of revolutions (5)
12 Backing food has a slight result (4)
15 Section with an unspecified number of men in it (7)
16 Space for throwing utensils into a river (7)
17 Go about a small coin to get some tasty food (3, 4)
19 Insular example of what comes from pigs in what comes from sheep (7)
21 She has her day once a year (4)
22 A good thing to have in hand for disposal of course (5)
23 Nothing to back a warm favourite with, what a depressing thing! (4)
26 An exact reference (7, 3, 5)
27 Sound part of fliers mostly (7)
28 Circuit completed from near the dynamo (7)

1 Their results are not always out in the field (7)
2 One of those two-horse-power affairs (8, 3, 4)
3 In the army it must be kept in munitions (4)
4 Half an empire is involved in this cricket business, causing such a storm (7)
5 Space-travel enthusiasts want to get away from this sort of thing (7)
6 Box one knocks up easily (4)
7 'Ring each morning' (anag.) (a loyal royal peal of course) (8, 7)
8 Can be held to be reversible island trap (7)
13 Lure finally shy (5)
14 Expression of contempt is turned around for a warrior (5)
17 Not a beautiful bird, but makes a nice pal (7)
18 Early paper that is late in a way (7)

50

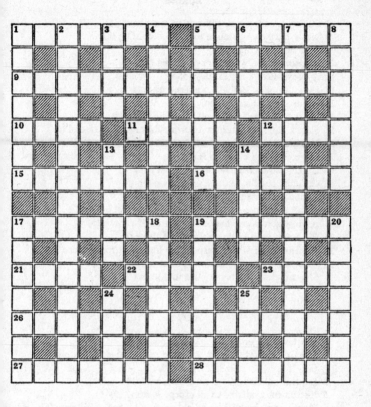

19 Colour that is meant to be a guide later (7)
20 Defer and see us shut up inside (7)
24 This man is used to being sat on (4)
25 When it takes a turn it is upset (4)

105

51

1 Skill in a sailor is so difficult to apprehend (6)
4 Not typical though quite usual to the rating (8)
9 In action, certainly (6)
10 Pleasant drink by itself or set in tea (8)
12 A province of Central Italy (5)
13 Forest donkey, perhaps obscured by it (4-5)
15 It introduces a single name (3)
16 River beginning of Carroll's fighting twins (5)
17 Strong liquor that brings its own punishment in the end (6)
20 Not an exciting thing to get into (3)
22 In he goes, self evident (3)
25 Conducted a part soundly for money (6)
26 Clean by soaking, little less than whiten (5)
29 Luminous bridge but the car is wrecked (3)
30 Is this Government formed to look after fuel? (9)
33 An instruction one may be honoured to receive (5)
34 But tours seem to be a source of temper (8)
35 A bit of housework is responsible for this chronic dance (6)
36 Meddled with some central current unit (8)
37 She can easily get herself tied in a knot (6)

1 What a small orchestra allows is poetry (8)
2 The Communist went on the stage and arranged for publication (8)
3 But this palace is not a royal residence (9)
5 Instrument available to all except Joseph? (5)
6 Place of rest from which to obtain an A1 signal of distress (5)
7 Came across a brick-carrier in the way (6)
8 The shelter was coloured and looked unpleasantly (6)
11 Politely perspires (6)
14 Draw a number over the torn bit (4)
18 This only puts off the evil day for the evil-doer (6)
19 Coal torch used in polishing glass (9)
21 Military force in punitive expedition (4)

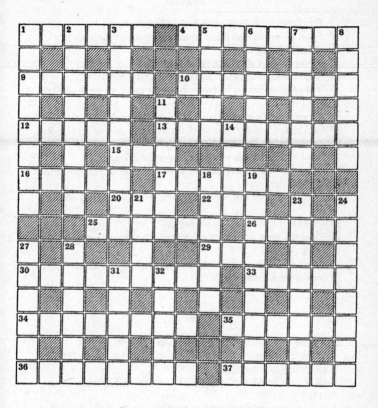

23 Fruity old-time Chinese dignitary? (8)
24 It supplies liquids and solids for home consumption by invalids (8)
27 An opening remark of some expense to a good balancer (6)
28 He doesn't carry much weight in boxing circles (6)
31 Habituate in a river (5)
32 After the matter has been 2 down this may appear (5)

52

1 To discover fish in what one excels in is lucky (9)
9 From it one may get sweet nourishment or just sweet air (6)
10 Ways ended in time (9)
11 A way that, in short, encloses a tree (6)
12 Unrestricted description of worn-out jumpers (9)
13 It is often subjected to blows and may cut a memorable figure (6)
17 A useful point to be heeded when taking one's cue (3)
19 Behind the scenes, attacks of these might lead to a theatrical display of 'the jitters'! (4-5, 6)
20 Food still shown on some of our copper coinage (3)
21 Not quite a representative of our Upper House in the centre of New York (6)
25 Its inauguration may be a capital affair on an entirely new line (9)
26 Name is not the same in France (6)
27 There's a certain amount of agitation for the provision of this drink (4, 5)
28 Weather comment certainly noisy enough in the interior (6)
29 It's rare in culinary circles (9)

2 The royal figure to which no robe could be fitted (6)
3 One type of occupation at least depends on his survival (6)
4 Lie snug and close (6)
5 'Star turn in A1 fog,' (anag.) (It certainly makes a big change) (15)
6 Perhaps they will be found to have been badly folded? (4, 5)
7 In numbers I have become concentrated (9)
8 A person so described cannot, presumably, commit high treason (9)
14 More than enough to eclipse a cake-walk? (9)
15 Metal with a bit over for waste (5-4)
16 Those who like to walk or drive on the level should try here (9)
17 Label for a sleeping fly-by-night (3)

18 Bird enclosure (3)
22 It could be used for raising heavy weights, or for bringing them down (6)
23 After a car smash he'd become bent! (6)
24 Said to be largely part of a wheel (6)

53

1 The real end to food for small children (3, 4)
5 Grown-up's name for 1 across collectively (7)
9 It was fruit that started the conflict (5)
10 Beheaded, the doctor would easily attend to this injury (7)
11 A Czech play (3)
12 One needs some sense to detect it (5)
13 People rarely enter by this door (9)
16 Someone to know in Scotland (3)
17 It meant a run in the old days (5)
18 This will make the engineer's E.M.F. go up (7)
20 Malay knives (7)
23 Anchor in arbour! (5)
26 Pass on which you may rightly pause (3)
27 The proper place for your money in a riverside town (5, 4)
31 It doesn't take the cake; the reverse is true (5)
32 Sounds like a boy of colour (3)
33 This guest never turns up unexpectedly (7)
34 A sensational sample? (5)
35 All in? No – this fat is on the animal's exterior (7)
36 Chaperones who start something owing to somebody! (7)

DOWN

1 Air to abstain from (7)
2 Gets information from a mine, perhaps (4, 3)
3 This sheepskin might have come from a star ruler in Asia (9)
4 Partly common sense but entirely confidential across the Channel (5, 4)
5 22 down with the French ending is a feature of a house (5)
6 Not to be trusted, not being upright (5)
7 Encourage feeding in a Hall near Chester (5)
8 It might apply paint in the finest possible way (7)
14 A city well known among marionettes (3)
15 Printers know this German river well (3)
18 Foolish fellow who must be divided and transposed for execution (9)

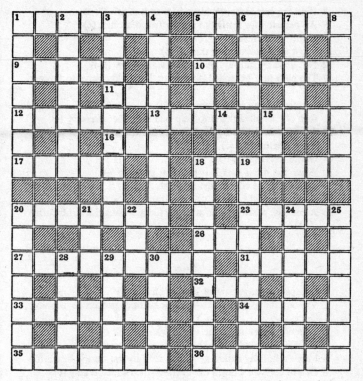

19 Prisoners put in here were out of sight, and of mind, often (9)
20 Not wholly biased (7)
21 A populated ford in Kent (3)
22 Said to be a gift to politicians! (3)
24 With sun it makes an enjoyable holiday (7)
25 Move back a little more than the way out (7)
28 Brides are, if away (5)
29 It may sum up the whole idea (5)
30 Stage wood, nearly red-hot (5)

54

ACROSS

8 If all the errand boys whistle it, then it is this (7, 3)
9 An occasion for festivities among frugal ascetics (4)
10 If this were an eagle . . . (4, 2, 4)
11 . . . it might even carry this off (4)
12 Not an early railway, but a marine life-saver (6-4)
17 The club that beheaded offers a national alternative to flowers (5)
20 Spotted among some loose ends (4)
21 It is often well situated to help one raise the necessary (4)
23 A pound in the bank, but do not offer this sort of a cheque on the strength of it! (5)
24 Oddfellows? (7, 3)
30 When the die is cast it is this that emerges (4)
31 Set foot repeatedly in the same place (6, 4)
32 The legally right sort of way to arrange a line (4)
33 A counsel, possibly, who is hardly likely to languish in obscurity (5, 5)

DOWN

1 Compact arrangement of broken images (5)
2 Various things point to a truth sometimes proved on washing day (8)
3 This old fellow might be useful with a hook (6)
4 Building a mixed bar with a chemist around (6)
5 Many a holiday-maker gets back to it to rest on the beach (6)
6 One of Captain Cook's discoveries which ended fatally (6)
7 The court jester's mock emblem (6)
13 It carries little weight in the animal kingdom (5)
14 A name of some eminence in South Africa (5)
15 To a physician it is something to cheat if possible (4)
16 At no time are things less shady than at this (4)
18 Getting it at golf is hardly playing to the gallery (4)
19 He was an Irish soldier or peasant (4)
22 A nuisance in the garden puts an insect in the clear (8)
24 Implement largely ill-made (6)

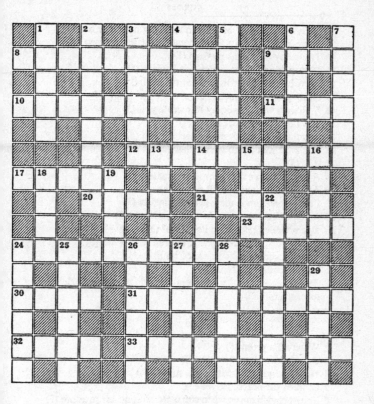

25 Winning it our cricketers erase more painful memories of the past (6)
26 A storm-tossed doctor elects to take his chance (6)
27 Putting up an edge on time is just an illusion (6)
28 Many a person has employed it to help with the rent (6)
29 Order a half-hedge in America (5)

55

1 He is not a pugilist but he can hand out a sock or two (11)
9 Success of a Roman figure coming in late confused (5)
10 Travel, by no means modern (11)
11 Money found when a drain is broken (5)
12 Say what Washington is if not the capital (5)
15 Nasty pests show such characteristic specimens (5)
17 A French word that may intoxicate you (3)
18 The furious driver of Kings (4)
19 Merchandise, and it may travel as such (5)
21 The swift alone possesses a claw (5)
22 3 D (5)
23 A bit of leather that is broken in parts (5)
26 All that remained with Pandora (4)
27 Being small, emphatic when hers is first (3)
28 A pack member not to be taken seriously (5)
30 Open-handed people do not reveal them (5)
33 An old official who may still be seen with a ruff (5)
35 Though leading it's careless of results (11)
36 It's a pleasure to stand (5)
37 Shouts about broken Powers and does not provide good journalism (6, 5)

2 Ward off a green (5)
3 Rejected no sign of danger (5)
4 Nothing in a dry boat? Fish, surely! (4)
5 Scot, of the beach, maybe (5)
6 They provide music when subjected to some air pressure (5)
7 Make a mistake and kiss the old gun (11)
8 These drinks may be handed up from one person to another (7-4)
12 Might this precede the haggis on the menu? (6, 5)
13 Not a restful place, though it seems a sweet one (5-3, 3)
14 Nears a breakdown, and merits it (5)
15 Sheep get up here (3)
16 Cease to be objective (3)
20 Speak derisively (5)

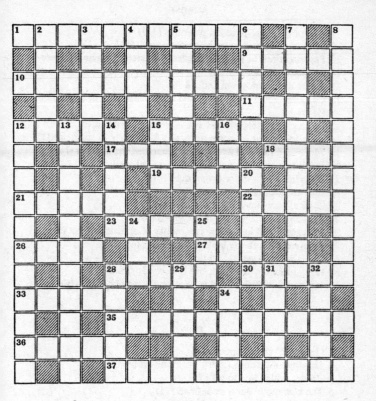

24 To love moreover or to embrace love (3)
25 Such adventure is perhaps archaic (3)
28 A water mole (5)
29 Peer but not look (5)
31 He may be married but not engaged (5)
32 Trials that are first set up (5)
34 Boat penny and how to get it (4)

56

1 One of these pre-prandial pleasures (3, 7)

9 Misnamed quiet dweller by the riverside (4)

10 Pay attentions to that which greatly interests woman, for ceremonious occasions (5, 5)

11 A city not unknown in Oxford (6)

12 Consume about seven score and a half, not without distinction (5)

15 For a change they should not be roughly handled (5)

18 Ever poetic that is shown to be of a kind likely to scare one (5)

19 More than material advice to one standing for election (7)

20 Put it in a wet-bob, and turn to a kind of relation (5)

21 She's just about in for bright quality (5)

22 Lies are used to apprehend (7)

23 Type of bore not met with ashore (5)

24 Lacking the second half of 10 across (5)

26 That many fall into decay is a matter of outside interest (5)

29 A severe critic in the building business? (6)

31 Choir takes to vegetarian dish (10)

32 It might send one to bed, but in bed it is stranded (4)

33 If a parcel with this label is kept long it may be high! (10)

DOWN

2 On this 29 across operates (4)

3 Upsurge of colourful spirit promotes crime (6)

4 Rather a high line to take (5)

5 The best motto for a tradesman? (5)

6 A leaf between leaves, perhaps (5)

7 Yet an expression the same in Scotland as a dairy product (10)

8 One would not look to it for the eye of a needle (7, 3)

13 The complete horseman (7)

14 What was said to live at the bottom of a well was certainly not in him (7)

15 Something to rest on in summer may be grand as tee, also (6, 4)

16 The packs that hunt them should, for lasting results, keep to pens rather than take the lead (10)

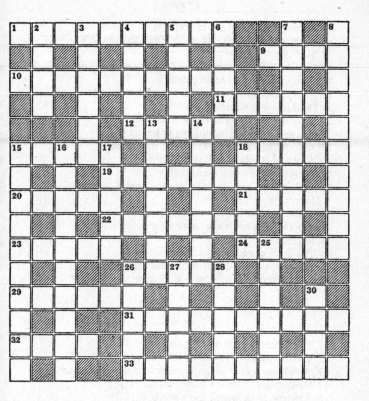

17 When a golfer is scratch he should do this well (5)
18 Foreign town that when led around was diminished (5)
25 She's a real eye-opener to early birds (6)
26 Bow turned to politician is a painful thing (5)
27 Part of 7 down, so to speak (5)
28 They could be very annoying to watch-dogs, of course! (5)
30 Fit source of water (4)

57

5 Letters, honourable and military (3)
8 Ancient place which gets rough about one hen (10)
9 To a this is exactly it (4)
10 Emboldened here, it may have been argued once (10)
11 Choice of letters to be used defensively (4)
12 To cry does a fat lot of good to the Eskimos! (7)
16 Once found in a general idea (7)
17 It attracts but to some extent is shy (5)
18 Examine softly with something to put on (5)
19 A signalling instrument for sound indoor use (5)
20 A man of Rome to us is really poison (5)
22 One of Napier's cats, perhaps (7)
23 The end has gone rapidly, its start goes back and all out of breath (7)
26 The stones that help you to keep going (4)
27 If the wingers are injured during the game, at least the team has this (6, 4)
30 The place in which he joins the sappers (4)
31 It is growing dark but there is some fragrance finally (10)
32 Sailor returns but this one doesn't when the ship founders (3)

1 Town from but not near 8 across (4)
2 This nation will give musical utterance (4)
3 With heart broken in Civil Defence though all mapped out (7)
4 Difficulties of having a horse on board (5)
5 A person to be looked up to at school (4, 3)
6 Warbler to be taken half jokingly (5-5)
7 Words picked up by this alone have a widespread audience (10)
10 Returning water from 12 across returning (3)
13 Agreeable offering to a traveller but it may be a difficult job (5, 5)
14 Evening worker popular with child photographers? (4-6)
15 Commit another crime, by gum! (5)
16 The god of revelry (5)

20 Rain upset in a large container is quite a different version (7)
21 Worked hard and finally passed out! (7)
24 Just a spot of money to a French bridegroom perhaps (3)
25 It has been customary for a long time with us (5)
28 A contrivance for river traffic. Would a quay undo it? (4)
29 Grand for some people, but not those in the docks (4)

ACROSS

1 It provides fair pickings to dip into (4, 3)
5 Shows mostly some kept out by Hadrian's wall (7)
9 Quittance in the matter of time for occupation (7)
10 Say a little good-bye to your tin, with music (7)
11 In the race for overseas trade Britain needs every one she can get, that's just horse sense! (9)
12 Before a meal it's bit by bit (5)
13 The line that James followed (5)
15 Quality, but a trite use for it (9)
17 Personal magnetism alone has done it, often (9)
19 A number up in bloom (5)
22 Cast, and its performance is energetic up North (5)
23 In train; the last part sounding like cattle (9)
25 A reprehensible affair, breaking our gate like that! (7)
26 State that played an active part at sea during the American Civil War (7)
27 The only one of seven made up of seven (7)
28 Sea change to look after an area in London (4, 3)

DOWN

1 One entitled upsets number or sailor (7)
2 Given permission for unlimited credit, apparently (7)
3 It might easily go to a lady's head (5)
4 It is often eaten in haste, and of course speedily ended (9)
5 This coin finally died out, though its end had several lives (5)
6 She may well be cut out for interior decorating! (3-2, 4)
7 Some talk over the French water gets a big build-up (7)
8 A tongue for the catty? (7)
14 It is hardly likely to be active in advance (9)
16 It might be a bit of a bore, or quite overwhelming (5, 4)
17 The fore part is aft, and the whole is a most unfriendly thing (7)
18 It grows this end up, naturally (7)
20 The soldier whose life never is! (7)
21 Human types vary from the highest to the lowest, and this is the mean (7)
23 Spirited, that is in young fish (5)
24 They are nothing to a slap up display of wealth (5)

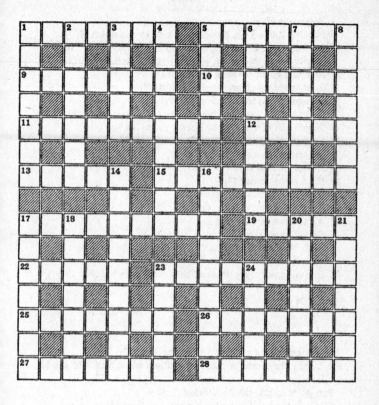

59

1 Bequeaths (6)
4 Possibly it is left up, though of a kind to run down (8)
9 Nothing turns back in it, but many seek health thereat (6)
10 Advice to the tradesman wishing to offer keen prices? (8)
12 It should be ample for a Canadian (5)
13 Partly unpleasant but wholly tuneful! (9)
15 A circuit provided by one sitting (3)
16 Feeling of an investor when a share has no interest for him? (5)
17 Simple sort of chap but he has the gift of oratory (4)
19 Love is another name for it (3)
21 No science to scare (3)
24 A bare tract of need (4)
25 Final word abroad (5)
28 In for it is 7 down in deed (3)
29 Smith gone crazy? Then do this! (9)
32 All this is a bewildering situation (2, 3)
33 Complimentary epithet for a baby (8)
34 With 36 across a London thoroughfare, scene of a great fire in 1861 (6, 6)
35 One may put up with their help, and even headless they get their livings (8)
36 See 34 across

1 Hamper with a good deal of colour in it (8)
2 Can be the means of smoothing stones and a fat lot of good it is! (8)
3 A guide to one-sided motoring (5, 4)
5 It is in the habit of answering airy questions (5)
6 Turns away in a particular direction (5)
7 Dividends frequently have two or more of it (6)
8 The best kind of news to get (6)
11 I've lost colour but stick it (6)
14 Part author of 23 down (4)
17 A building put together a long time after fish (6)
18 Attend a boxing match as some sailors do (4, 5)

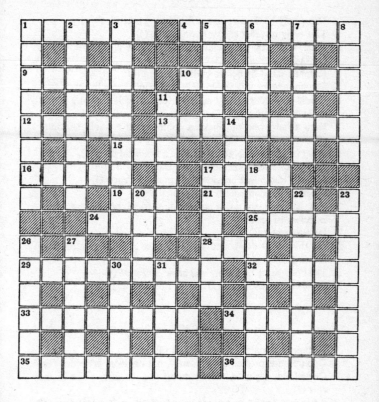

20 The extent of a small (very small!) Scots island (4)
22 How to get back your loss in a dive – melt it! (8)
23 I buy a rat from Persia (8)
26 It makes you and me competent to be of some service (6)
27 Put in prison (6)
30 Put it with 28 across and mum's the word (5)
31 This man clamours for regular appeasement (5)

60

1 There may be divers reasons for staying here (5, 5)
9 This early traveller certainly was game (4)
10 Their wrongful manipulation might cause a collapse of the banks (5-5)
11 Knight's stand-by before battle is joined (6)
12 The hounds for this would be bloodhounds, very likely (3-4)
15 Would it yield greenery suitable for a circular wreath that is to be cast overboard? (7)
16 Even a baby one can make a contribution towards harmony (5)
17 What is usual in a bottle may have a fine head on it (4)
18 Its growth owed something to Sir Isaac Newton (4)
19 A group that might provide some punch, of sorts (5)
21 When they become seedy they soon die (7)
22 Not carrying so much weight but some people are much exercised to get it (7)
24 Do a stretch? (6)
27 Do this to 19 down and you will have a real poser on your hands (10)
28 The body being this, there will be no sensation (4)
29 Wine of this description is usually home-made (5-5)

2 It stages a popular rising in Egypt (4)
3 One up on expressed unpopularity, but no more is needed (6)
4 Curtail this repeated movement to put the little horse in the cart (7)
5 After marriage they are apt to enter into one's calculations of course (4)
6 Secured in such a way as to be relieved from an awkward spot (7)
7 Quite satisfied at first, but developing into active discord (10)
8 Easy pace about a warm place for a seventeenth-century Scot (10)
12 A fellow quite well off, one would say (3, 2, 5)

124

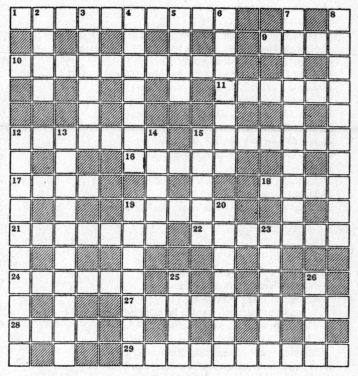

13 Nearly too late, a devil of a close thing! (4, 2, 4)
14 Among them are to be found the oldest of living things (5)
15 If there were pig races this would be first home, and last out (5)
19 Flat iron that is heated for use (7)
20 Is his dishonest success due to his being able to cut the cards
 more effectively than others? (7)
23 It's safest when lifeless, if you grasp what I mean (6)
25 A Scotland Yard creation that can turn blue to red (4)
26 One worthy of the spotlight? (4)

61

1 Gallicized tenor oboe (3, 7)

9 A tyrant in fine robes (4)

10 It helps to illuminate the underground (6, 4)

11 Quite a draught but nothing to do with open doors (6)

12 These are cables not telegrams (7)

15 Foretell the colour in an ancient northerner (7)

16 Rouse a sailor in the middle of the street (5)

17 The number thrown for any number of players (4)

18 This island sounds like a bit of heaven (4)

19 The best part (5)

21 It's slaty in mixture, but very good (7)

22 It is more than a wonder this poet existed (7)

24 Revelry (6)

27 Equivalent to that which is required here (10)

28 Once this began many a tale (4)

29 'Trust an ear' (anag.) (to learn what's cooking?) (10)

2 Shape of a circle with some value (4)

3 Natural forces or human factors (6)

4 Springs in many bathrooms (7)

5 It would be extremely hard if he preceded a little worker (4)

6 Take some wine to give strength (7)

7 Plant a fairy sea-snail (10)

8 Slovenly result of neglecting the cobbler (4-2-4)

12 A juggler's formula is absolute deception (5-5)

13 Not up to cleaning capital (10)

14 This account is given in the history books (5)

15 Father of Paris (5)

19 Get-together of a hundred with different result (7)

20 A heavenly body à la wine (7)

23 Six proceed to an old city in vital force (6)

25 Refreshing places in which advocates may work (4)

26 It gives a timely idea to compose some article on (4)

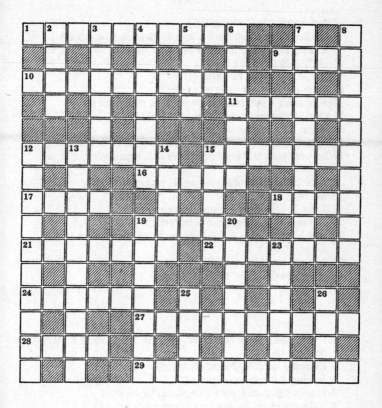

62

1 A fish that is never caught (7)

5 Military force says it has the right to do some salvaging (7)

9 A crazy suggestion for night fliers and where to find them, too (4, 2, 3, 6)

10 Joseph, the young kangaroo (4)

11 Extra payment put on in a vehicle (5)

12 If you seek a positive sign, do not look under this (4)

15 Could irritation from it cause a blister? (7)

16 Room for outfit number and bird (7)

17 An active fellow who hopes to be first in the field (7)

19 Eminent artist is literary director as well, apparently, and is well spoken of (7)

21 A fat colleague of this kind would be destructively representative (4)

22 Some flowers from Neptune's garden? (5)

23 The man to hold back the waters (4)

26 'No moon Henry? Gift!' (anag.) (the burglar's dream, it's just too easy!) (5, 3, 7)

27 Red sets into fruit, possibly (7)

28 Showing evidence of many tears? (3-4)

1 If you don't know of a week with this label, ask a scout to help you (3-1-3)

2 Evidently not side-tracked (2, 3, 5, 5)

3 Journey that can be upsetting (4)

4 Interesting opening for a keen young terrier (3-4)

5 Animal representing headless Indian ox in stone (7)

6 Lord of the 16 across (4)

7 In the full flower of activity and health? (2, 5, 2, 1, 5)

8 Early one day in Spring (3, 4)

13 Fish canonized as metal (5)

14 Crumble toast for an animal (5)

17 Agitated certainly, but not defenceless finally (7)

18 The act of some former form of pilot? (7)

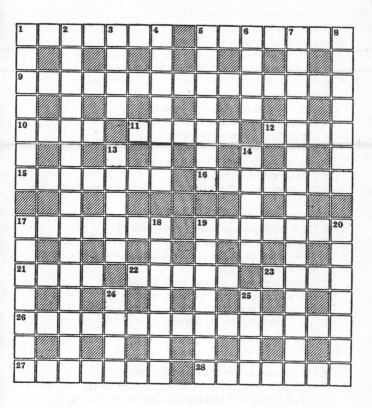

19 He will certainly have designs (7)
20 Embankment no longer new is no longer unimpaired (7)
24 Ancient town involved in present day revolutions (4)
25 Standing aid to sportsmen in the field (4)

63

1 One can have a sit-down wash in it, it seems, though really pushed for personal conveyance (4, 5)

6 A thousand in deep sleep only making a short stop (5)

9 An instrument you can get from no axe-shop (9)

10 Famous old king in a modern vehicle can't be real (5)

11 A beetle puts the perch back (3)

12 Collections, that is, found in big eels (9)

15 It is very sweet and sounds as if it might be my solo (5)

16 The graduate Augustus is a sorcerer (5)

19 Like some Bach work, for instance, all frowsty at the start (5)

21 Employment is never without you and me in it (3)

22 Take up a false position? (3)

23 Its commercial progress may be subject to control from the bank (5)

24 But this hair is a useful support (5)

26 Use a rag to produce an out-of-date coin (5)

27 An ancient British title, enough to make a writer be tedious (9)

31 To be taken in by the nostrils and given out audibly by the mouth sometimes (3)

32 He with such copying might make a pile (5)

33 How a neat tiger might put things together (9)

35 Units of the forces found dates here in the last war! (5)

36 One of the combinations that makes the Scottish reel (9)

1 Learned men and numbers are fundamental (5)

2 Bully beef, perhaps, but not fit for consumption (5)

3 Put everything back into this wood and it will give way (5)

4 A verve that is past (3)

5 The class of instruments to which 9 across belongs (5)

6 The vehicle a South American city allowed to be a car (9)

7 To be of the first kind denotes importance (9)

8 They act for others but not upon a stage (9)

13 Animal hung upside down and curtailed (3)

14 To conclude with a negative might indeed be hell (5)

16 A large number bring into line a busy worker of evil intent (9)

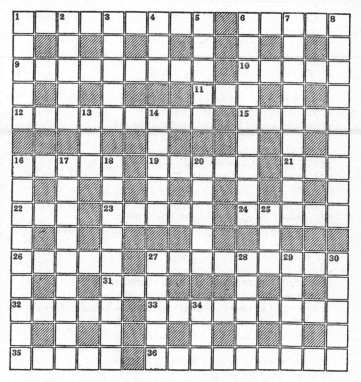

17 This style is the new style – in dates not dresses (9)
18 Foreign footwear grows old and does much damage (9)
20 A safe colour to go on (5)
25 The Shop, as initially known (3)
27 A soft coating of frost for the best kind of joint (5)
28 Conservative estimation of what's due? (5)
29 A natural or artificial fertilizer (5)
30 Relative arrangement of penitence unconfined (5)
34 Animal from 33 across (3)

64

ACROSS

1 One cannot say that this place is not a patch on a pleasant face (6, 4)
8 To do so would ruin the act (6)
9 In place of pictures there's bitterness in a blood carrier (3, 7)
10 A creature coming back very thin (6)
11 Having illuminating ups and downs, perhaps (10)
12 Form of rental accounting for some overhead points (6)
13 Fabulous figure by means of self (4)
15 Perhaps a good blow could make it rise? (4, 3)
19 Open to conviction or a free issue (2, 5)
21 The boss claiming the Derby winners? (4)
22 Extensive opening with horse partly filling it (3, 3)
25 Each night disturbed, that's all (10)
27 A thing bent with pain, and extremely chilly (6)
28 Died cut up about finite change but not unknown (10)
29 A famous conqueror at the beginning (6)
30 They have been known to warn tramps away from bars (10)

DOWN

1 A small thing to drive, and a place to cross, in Yorks (8)
2 With an end in view, to do so is satisfying (6)
3 One might give them beheaded to a knitter, and receive them (6)
4 All the world has a place in this system (5)
5 Another three scored, but don't be satisfied yet (3, 5)
6 The injury it causes might be dressed with the middle of it (8)
7 Form of paean unhappy inside, in America (8)
13 Opportunely Hibernian (3)
14 One might get a useful line from its tip (3)
16 Finally leave the home fires which burn in the final part (8)
17 Still welcoming a master? Surely not! (4, 4)
18 A particular combination of cape and isle (8)
20 'L.s.d. on dog' (anag.) (a lucrative win if it comes home!) (4, 4)
23 I'm up among the heavenly bodies, so I must have negotiated a big flight! (6)
24 It has associations both atomic and revealingly anatomic! (6)
26 A stock feature of Western America (5)

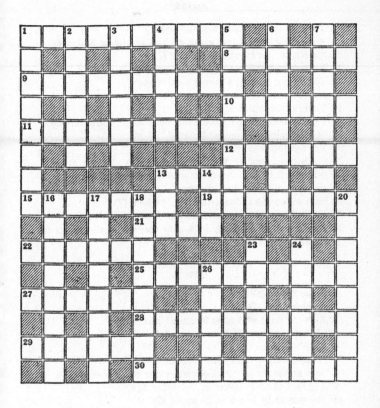

65

1 They are submerged in various ways (6)
4 A flier that gives details about a knock-out in the States (6)
10 Started fast, go on after in the East (7)
11 You are certainly not in this if on holiday (7)
12 To this one nothing becomes a brave man (3)
13 Playful means of stirring our emotions? (5)
14 Many at the back find it dull (5)
15 How Gilbert's Lord High Executioner liked to be treated (13)
18 ' Grace grabs pet ' (anag.) (6-7)
23 The Spanish open poetically but run away (5)
25 Easily spent on a day of victory in a tree (5)
26 With the R.N. it shows direction and not without it (3)
27 Entrance of a grim Italian river (7)
28 Seen with a gag and takes on hand perhaps (7)
29 But in Latin took nourishment with a settled result (6)
30 People used to sit quietly in it, now they act in all manner of ways! (6)

1 Make fun of (6)
2 A game point (7)
3 She's the artist who takes in a brick-carrier (5)
5 First-class colour will become ventilated (5)
6 12.30 to a sailor . . . (3, 4)
7 . . . and his poetical eye can take in much (6)
8 Even an acrobatic defrauder cannot turn this, however (2, 6, 5)
9 A growth much in favour in December (9, 4)
16 The tree to be found in 25 across (3)
17 To be prone to falsehood? (3)
19 Stirred up and employed the end (7)
20 Went mad about an air gunner with damaging results (7)
21 with 25 down. Classic inscription often seen on timepieces (6, 5)
22 Quickly coming from 27 across curtailed (6)
24 A mostly smooth occurrence (5)
25 See 21 down

66

ACROSS

1 Knocking back drink can start them, and they're hot (7)
5 If you cannot afford an umbrella, you can at least run to this (7)
9 Poetic and repetitive instruction for surf and snooker (5, 5, 5)
10 Clay instrument (4)
11 Natural spectacles that may get one down (5)
12 It takes more than one to play it as a game (4)
15 This is not intended to be an aid to deserting a sinking ship (7)
16 Wood closely grown at the front (7)
17 For features on feet reverse one spot in another one (3-4)
19 Make a record going out? (4, 3)
21 A stopper, or starting one under the bonnet (4)
22 Some may have a fighting chance of getting this drunk (5)
23 Valley contribution to England, and ignored (4)
26 A bright show on the garden front (9, 6)
27 It might be instructive, or reproving (7)
28 Make good strides to manage a water supply (3, 4)

DOWN

1 Descriptive of the pipes, as a rule (7)
2 Being this these days helps many stately homes to keep going (4, 2, 3, 6)
3 Usually taken as meaning black, but could be of different colours (4)
4 An expert in the water, but an outsider (7)
5 For a colourful result, let's change and put the car in (7)
6 A waterway that is to be under the Spanish (4)
7 Arboreal feature of Eden (4, 2, 9)
8 Take our way to deal with dead fires (4, 3)
13 A den put up with a few inside to try to equal (5)
14 Not very bright-looking (5)
17 What is got out of a clay pit can be representative (7)
18 Change the order and prevaricate (7)
19 Lasting for an age it may be civil (7)
20 An occasion for sorrow (7)
24 He was responsible for a black day for British arms (4)
25 From being this to ceasing to be is life (4)

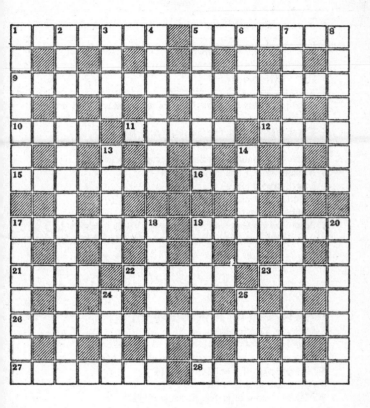

67

1 Rank meadow official? (5, 7)
8 State of a graduate at heart (7)
9 The blows stern men suffer? (7)
12 Reproduce with acid drops, perhaps (4)
13 Game to stir up warmth (5)
14 A painter with a bit of dark and light in him (4)
17 Distinguish between something round and flat and the northern end (7)
18 The shadow of time may be seen on its face (3-4)
19 Ring writer starts a gap (7)
22 It can be wounding to refuse to recognize a girl (7)
24 A diagram of a learner in a vessel (4)
25 Utterly stupid (5)
26 A notion that just is not perfect (4)
29 A ruminant on the extreme left? (3, 4)
31 Bring into confusion some embrocation with a lubricant (7)
32 'Let all MS rest' (including little missives?) (anag.) (5, 7)

1 This fellow shows I am in the money (7)
2 Made up, Dutch fashion (4)
3 A monster swallows nothing, just like a soldier (7)
4 Such solutions are not confined to chemistry (7)
5 Separate part of a holiday resort (4)
6 Rising fish in shelter (3)
7 A B.B.C. monitor is one, for example (12)
10 Right dress, in one of the Services (5)
11 Indecision of almost identical words: join up (6-6)
15 Hutton not out! Revered by the Soviet (5)
16 It breaks one French combine (5)
20 Dash'd creature! (5)
21 Certainly common and not up to 1 across (7)
22 Quite happy to study the canvas (7)
23 Energetic couples of artistes appearing in the centre (7)

27 In good spirits due to spring, no doubt (4)
28 A bit of blending is obviously quite clever (4)
30 M-m-m-measuring units in print (3)

ACROSS

1 A teacher in different and feminine guise (9)
8 A message to a hydro marquee should protect your idea (7, 6)
11 Wants to be born, the cash follows (5)
12 It is for a doctor to admit – to do it is to die (5)
13 Country ones may be an asset in a way but not always to their owners (5)
16 What one might do with children who lose money and are upset (6)
17 Try to catch a candidate out before he is in, perhaps (6)
18 Eccentric way of getting rid of engineers (5)
19 The chance sometimes taken by a trespasser in the farmer's field? (4-2)
20 Leaves, and starts off by the river (6)
21 Support for a pompous person maybe (5)
24 Such an object if distant is of little value today (5)
26 A popular series of movements in Vienna (5)
27 Scott called her Ellen – why not Lily? (4, 2, 3, 4)
28 A boy's name with a cape hides nothing (9)

DOWN

2 In choral work they are not top-liners (5)
3 An obstacle some just take in their stride (6)
4 He was fictitiously associated with Hentzau (6)
5 Observed to be like music (5)
6 'Cable prisoner' (anag.) (7-6)
7 Amateurish and at times a striking description (13)
9 A tin estate, maybe, but who is to own it? (9)
10 Sub-standard, perhaps (5, 4)
13 Plant on board where stocks are kept (5)
14 Appearances at this often result in girls leaving home (5)
15 A protective covering may come from these (5)
22 A quarrel in an Indian dining room? (6)
23 Childish marine growth (6)
25 Ever in the centre, altogether jollier (5)
26 The land raised by the whip? (5)

68

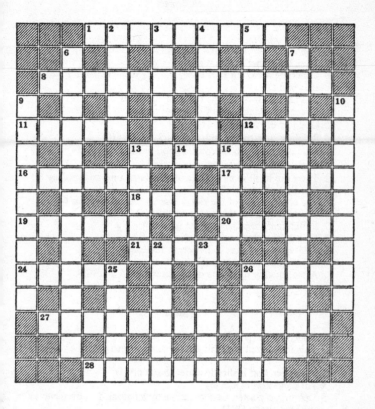

69

1 A dashing lover from poetry who owed his name to water and nickel steel (9)
6 One feature of a face that turns another one up (5)
9 To sell toys made from it might be thought a burning shame (9)
10 Generally speaking it is dead, but dig around it for speaking at length (5)
11 Animal that includes the home of 10 across (9)
14 Has anyone claimed that flying saucers come from here? (5)
15 Goddess of youth at the bar (4)
16 Building constructed with a politician inside (6)
19 Mounted on a cob it provides good pickings for many races (5)
20 In reduced circumstances it is worked by a forger (4, 3)
22 There are large numbers in a small island, one cannot deny (5)
23 Use the hypodermic? (6)
24 The contribution of the rhinoceros to a famous circus (4)
26 The willing horse that needs no spur (5)
27 In different shape has spent a game (9)
32 Gazelle characterized by Shakespeare (5)
33 Trifling in argument in irrelevant fashion (9)
34 A little one, commonly (5)
35 A nice quality too much or too little would mar (9)

1 Ended by the law, it is clear (5)
2 This instrument is nothing more than a restraint to evil-doers (5)
3 Accustom that is shortly about to run up (5)
4 An orchestral bloom (5)
5 Colouring matter that causes a revolutionary movement in military circles (3, 3)
6 They come from an open clime and are admittedly wonderful! (9)
7 Undoubtedly a crime of relative enormity (9)
8 There would no doubt be ample grounds for his appointment (9)
12 One who is responsible for deeds (4)
13 Wine for dinner, and the bird included (7)
16 To inquire about the farm vehicle, on the breakfast table (9)
17 Well preserved, but bound to be buried as a rule (9)

18 Exactly as the words imply it is a later composition in flower (9)
21 Dweller in green mansions backs an Eastern ruler (4)
25 Light may be thrown on glass described thus, but not with penetrating results (6)
28 A common growth little by little if curtailed (5)
29 There's something on foot rising to degrees (5)
30 If you do not want this, not a word (5)
31 Gives one's name in symbols (5)

ACROSS

1 Might be Oxford or Cambridge for instance or even Maidstone (6, 4)
8 Diarist who might name the girl (6)
9 The lower deck begin departing secretly (10)
10 Objecting to a Gaelic conclusion? (6)
11 One who thinks another's ideas worth taking (10)
12 Put into words a tied in arrangement (6)
13 A city in a pro-Slovak region (4)
15 Love starts such a destructive process (7)
19 Cover showing final decay (7)
21 Is your heart this at times when you pay it? (4)
22 No middle here but put an ear into the middle to make it all attractive (6)
25 People kindly make them though they may be spent (10)
27 A garment to move sharply in (6)
28 A broken underground approach in time should come to frighten (10)
29 Enormous creatures, as children call them (6)
30 May be a shout under but in fact like a clap above (10)

DOWN

1 Was it an epic play that produced smoke? (4, 4)
2 Get an M.P. off his high horse, perhaps! (6)
3 One of those lines of latitude the French think mostly too much (6)
4 The kind of rose you may find in a stud or coat of armour (5)
5 A complete denial for example in a race (8)
6 The little black boy thought he stopped ships bumping! (8)
7 Sit so back with nothing between? My head! What a blooming result! (8)
13 The number mainly taken into consideration by the selfish (3)
14 To do this alone is not to interfere (3)
16 Rennur came second? (6-2)
17 'Sits by K.C.' (anag.) (and gives him support?) (6, 2)
18 If he goes to church, he may do voluntary work (8)

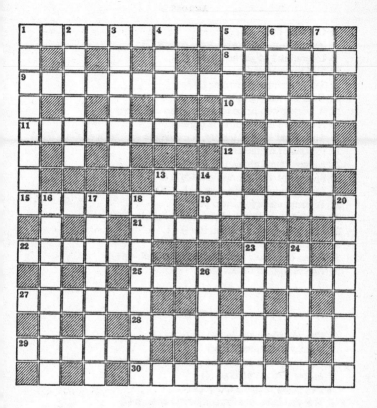

20 Peg in a bundle of hay for those who look after (8)
23 The bag is in a glen (6)
24 Is it a suitable sheet of paper for a composer to use? (6)
26 An opinion free from a Greek letter may be malodorous to some (5)

71

1 Growing fruit (11)
7 Some Great Dane exploded a banger (7)
8 Liberation? Might be a catch (7)
10 Nicely made ox (4)
11 Sat to arrange the ermine (5)
13 Used for fencing in the deep eels (4)
15 A worker who helps to make up an anthology (3)
17 A colour smeared in 15 is burning (6)
19 An ancient king of history, for example see the beginning (6)
20 It depends on the listener (3-4)
21 Digger, round about 100, gets the chopper (6)
23 Spotted part of the masquerade? (6)
25 Cuban dances always start with it (3)
27 Payment made for a tear (4)
28 Bowled short like the French of Switzerland (5)
29 Unless turning in around is! (4)
32 One way to get positive results (7)
33 It can contribute toward a highway hook-up (7)
34 Agrees with sentiment (11)

DOWN

1 Can plaid be made in two colours? (7)
2 Starchy repast, maybe (4)
3 Place for those on the run on the Continent (6)
4 A cow catcher, perhaps (6)
5 Not pretty, like the Gorgons (4)
6 This specimen was formerly quite enough (7)
7 Law-enforcers overseas (11)
9 Bunch of domestic bulbs (11)
12 Nero's in it, causing trouble (7)
14 Being born in the southern region, gives a derisive smile (5)
16 Encourage bird food and have no rising (3, 2)
18 Viscid and liquid bluejacket (3)
19 For a result this is the limit (3)
22 Reduce to perplexity (7)

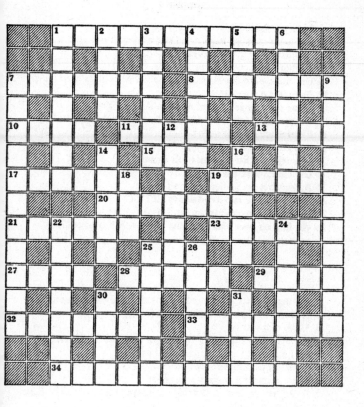

24 They depend sometimes on trees and always on climate (7)
25 Arrived with an artist to take pictures (6)
26 One way to spoil some champagne – boil, perhaps (6)
30 Get a drink for a medico in the morning (4)
31 Music from the New World (4)

72

1 Loan car for a Mohammedan book (7)
5 Animal, vegetable, mineral? Have a try at it (4)
9 Ruler to be in the direct line, perhaps (4, 2, 3, 6)
10 A little whirlpool is set up in mixed dyes (4)
11 One finds a number demand this vessel without its head (5)
12 If so, it is a fact (4)
15 Came out as a reversal of many in degree (7)
16 Uninteresting joker, not likely to help one to be bright (4, 3)
17 Fixed snare of light fame (7)
19 Wander around with average Communist backing (7)
21 A party to inflict only on one's enemies (4)
22 Difficulties with a horse on board (5)
23 A character on the musical staff (4)
26 Martian riches may be, one day (10, 2, 3)
27 A legal suspension for support (4)
28 An English poet who holds the wherewithal to write (7)

1 Having two articles allowed within one, he is certainly active (7)
2 Nanny, not of the 5 across variety (9, 5)
3 Value of a tear (4)
4 Annoyed by being quite a few up at first, but finally led (7)
5 Had a shot in the dark, one might say (7)
6 It's some pain in a cheek (4)
7 Tense commentary on our times (7)
8 A feather or two in our caps perhaps, used to give a false impression (8, 6)
13 It is not to be suffered easily, though the start is past (5)
14 There's nothing in the home, so we'll have to remain on water (5)
17 His scientific discoveries were remarkable, in so distant a time (7)
18 The works where a girl got in to try (7)
19 They helped 17 down in current inducements (7)

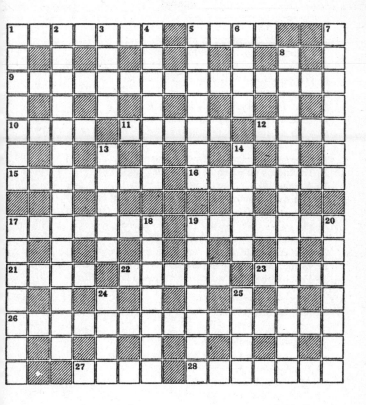

20 He made the sappers much better, apparently (7)
24 There's nothing in the wee home for a bird (4)
25 A good landsman for a sailor to be (4)

ACROSS

2 See 10 across
8 Implement excessive to a learner (4)
9 Honest instrument for people of good tone (7, 5)
10 With 2 across. Drive this to send hither and thither (4, 6, 2, 4)
12 It is quite usual to do this with oakum (5)
14 Big blow which puts the second letter at the end (5)
17 Refuse to start and finish official (5)
18 Some who do it endanger their wings! (3, 2)
19 With 18 down. A present time figure, popular with children (5, 5)
20 A body of live men nearly a dead one (5)
21 The town with which he can become pagan (5)
22 A resin (5)
23 This style of painting calls for a new form of green (5)
26 Give attention to the senior N.C.O. or get a black mark maybe (5)
30 A unique occurrence in a concert (4)
32 'Ben grips Kate' (going over a bridge?) (anag.) (8, 4)
33 Of little account to sappers yielding a bit of ground (4)
34 Fabulous but with some basis of reason finally (12)

DOWN

1 Just men according to Wallace (4)
2 This fruit with time will keep birds warm (4)
3 Inedible grub (5)
4 Clay from dear Gilbert (5)
5 Cricketer's gallery? (4)
6 Call in an uphill circuit to produce a bottle (5)
7 They used to take account of time in olden days (5)
10 So to golf, if the route march is broken up (4-4)
11 Occasionally, like a bad horseman! (3, 3, 2)
12 Can lees be used to remove dirt? (7)
13 A vessel given up for sauce (5)
14 He knows the law and a cross one will be impartial (7)
15 This city has been dear to many a Scot (8)

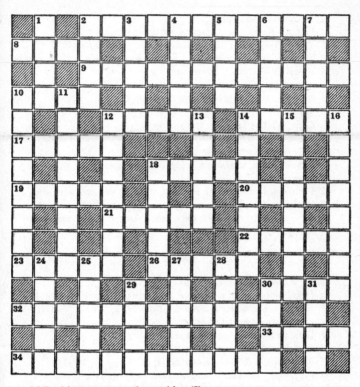

16 In this manner, rarely speaking (8)
18 See 19 across
24 This bird is usually well fed (5)
25 Part of a river which may stretch quite a way (5)
27 A giant mostly on the qui vive (5)
28 A gig leading would make this caper enormous (5)
29 One is often well-advised to swallow it whole (4)
30 Nothing to lap up here but stone (4)
31 Buoyant seaport (4)

74

8 A capital person abroad (8)

9 Jack the Killer, perhaps, often the cause of tears (6)

10 Many engaged in gathering activity, damaging woods (8)

12 Showing courage, mostly in a fighting situation (6)

14 A bull never is likely to be hurt (10)

18 He did not miss his fruit, they say (4)

21 A crime I and some police plead about (7)

22 Where many reports originate (3-4)

23 Their shooting season is fairly early (4)

25 Art is to any fashion as still here (10)

28 Only the not-outs can do it (6)

30 Benefits from someone's suggestion are sometimes obtained through it (8)

32 There's a passing word for him, if he is the one who goes there (6)

33 He was one of the musketeers, and is automatically due for a change (8)

DOWN

1 Some sweet thing arising from a couch (6)

2 John reminds us of a one-time parliamentary group in spirit (6)

3 If twice upset might be a pet dog (4)

4 Close fitting reversal of arms (4)

5 Comfortable spot for a little rest? (6)

6 'Tis about to tear up in animation (6)

7 Put troops in to exercise control (4)

11 Most easily attainable, and are in place of eggs (7)

13 They may end by liking a play, though showing bitterness at first (7)

14 Easily noticeable if one keeps one's eyes open (7)

15 It's when he loses heart that he becomes fat (5)

16 One way out of a complex itinerary (4)

17 Taking things like this is not a serious action (7)

19 A plant found in the Americas (5)

20 Turn this to transform (4)

24 Do it to learn the lie of the land (6)

74

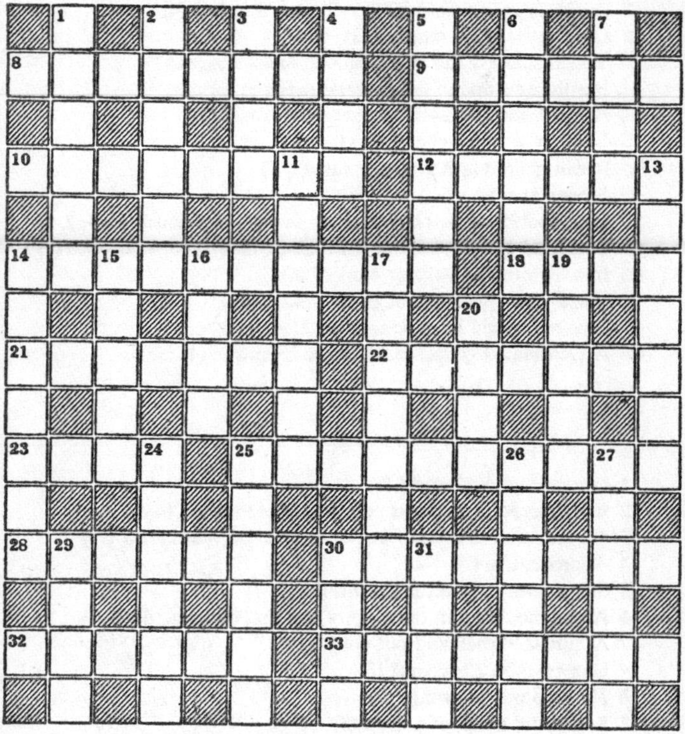

25 Firm never without tea (6)
26 One of the very simple doughboys? (6)
27 Was set upright, nevertheless is in an expensive turnover (6)
29 Money to take note of (4)
30 To avoid this fit of petulance, keep away from draughts (4)
31 Direction for action that is pressing (4)

75

8 A plucky man who might smoke when in bed (4)
9 On a letter it's a number (3)
10 You should get this eventually (2, 4)
11 Martha was one of his operatic heroines (6)
12 A lively condition – a few have it in Italy (8)
13 Literally a shifty character (3, 6, 6)
15 It will make tea last at any rate (2, 5)
17 Swastikas (7)
20 Four-footed animals clearly don't live so precariously (4, 4, 2, 5)
23 This kind of complaint doesn't attack many people at once (8)
25 In which the non-skater works? (6)
26 Vessel even poetic, though still illicit (6)
27 This red would have been made black (3)
28 A German song that cannot have been true (4)

1 Often drunk with toast (6)
2 Indication of a snake as seen from the towpath (4-4)
3 All the same to be achieved only when off one's feet? (15)
4 Apprehensive (7)
5 Some titles to celebrate in this list (8, 7)
6 Accommodation in the piggery was first designated (6)
7 A mite disturbed and put out (4)
14 Convey food 20 across? (3)
16 No herb put in storage (3)
18 Sound not much of a drop (8)
19 Train carrying old money (7)
21 Result of joint action in the business world? (6)
22 The correct thing to take on the bus – that's it (6)
24 Professionals, in a small way (4)

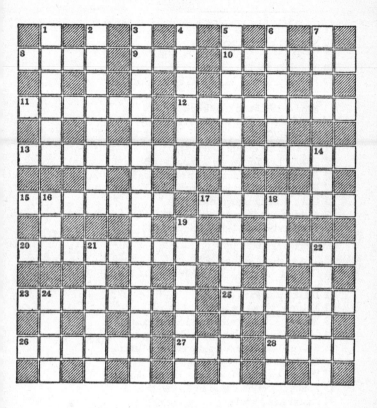

76

1 A Roman figure is not above the top, the stupid fellow (10)
8 A young bird of prey (6)
9 Knaves clutch a part of the neck like a coxcomb (10)
10 The earl's heavenly clockwork model (6)
11 Not very exciting, has a hole in the middle (10)
12 Battle grounds are to north – like following (6)
13 How to talk like a Continental pet (4)
15 This building goes round and round (7)
19 Sky-blue (7)
21 Give out the time in reverse (4)
22 Firmly fixed for beastly occupation (6)
25 Disguise made with a square somehow (10)
27 What is sometimes hoisted amidships? Cakes! (6)
28 Gave warning with menaces (10)
29 Fight of a packaged abstainer (6)
30 Transport is included – all checked (10)

1 Breakfast in Paris (8)
2 This silver is an alloy (6)
3 Brown, perhaps, in the Spanish hard coat (6)
4 Upon which the editor's circulation depends (5)
5 Solitary, sole but confused breaking a date (8)
6 Give rage its turn to distress (8)
7 The craven fellow from Crete ran like this (8)
13 Familiar Scot returns to an English river (3)
14 Assent was probably given to this deed (3)
16 It may be easier for some to see through his handiwork (8)
17 Polish is need for such manners (8)
18 His arbitration is peculiar to I.o.M. (8)
20 Prolonged and formerly looked after (8)
23 She figured among the big guns . . . (6)
24 . . . and was a well known this (6)
26 Search for the answer in the question (5)

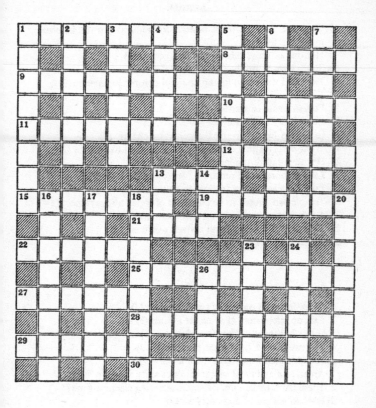

ACROSS

1 They are held to be a pattern for natural growth in some manly circles (6-4)
6 Not one of those shrewd turf characters! (4)
10 Stock term is productive of capital (5)
11 They find their own kind a study of consuming interest (9)
12 Type of soil to a greater degree used of old to destroy life (8)
13 Fourth estate in a crowd (5)
15 Food foray by 11 across? (3-4)
17 In fiction he experienced a generous change (7)
19 What deserves this description must remain to be seen (7)
21 Hardly a lad of the lower classes (7)
22 Late authoress of French and Russian affirmatives (5)
24 Low class subject of interest to cattlemen (8)
27 Temple too altered to be an object of superstitious respect (5-4)
28 A fair feature that goes on foot if curtailed (5)
29 This sort of thing is certainly not overdone (4)
30 The one at the top usually has it (10)

DOWN

1 Shop-damaged output of small jumpers (4)
2 Run up supporters of arms for infants (9)
3 Justly beheaded to become vigorous (5)
4 Retreat from a promising position (4, 3)
5 A sudden shot may give them a start (7)
7 An artist may take it of a studio to use its anagram in (5)
8 These studs make familiar sights at spring cleaning time (4-6)
9 How to get rid of a collection? (8)
14 It could put you on the scent of road repairs (5, 2, 3)
16 Rebelliously true of 2 down, often (2, 2, 4)
18 Cut back to correct what is this (9)
20 Steam is this form of water (7)
21 To be before is mostly to go back (7)
23 This change is alternate (5)
25 For an artist to make an offer is far from sensible (5)
26 Vehicle three-quarters full of fodder (4)

ACROSS

5 Nothing done in it can be concealed (6)
8 If you want to be big in heart, don't disparage others thus (8)
9 Some play them first and stand them after (6)
10 To find a raid fun could mean one is courageous (8)
11 What is spent is not in song (6)
12 When such a judgement is reversed the negative is sugar-coated (8)
15 Where to go to the pictures, possibly (5)
16 Making dishonest profit on the stock? (8)
19 A real scorcher to paint! (4-4)
24 He has a brush up first, and a wash later (5)
27 The literary notable who turned inquisitive at the last (8)
28 Skinny-headed couple of cats (6)
29 Often the cause of a hold-up at sea (8)
30 A third of a cigarette and a drink for one variety of the cicada (6)
31 Beat in altered limit in aggressive mood (8)
32 A reckoning for the 5 across (6)

DOWN

1 One mixture in dishes that is floral (7)
2 It would hardly do to fence with! (3-4)
3 Fat rent is in wrong (7)
4 What is divine in existence comforts one at night (7)
5 Arbour built by setting up a log (7)
6 Bit about a broken instrument that flies (4-3)
7 Tie in a tavern as the breath of life must be (7)
13 Feline circle known in ancient Rome (4)
14 It's on top of the world (4)
17 Is it the toady of the animal world? (4)
18 A side-splitter in point of time (4)
20 One different in the row is beastly noble (7)
21 Depressing occasions for outsiders? (3, 4)
22 There's no point in effort of this description (7)
23 One of the great rulers of Egypt (7)

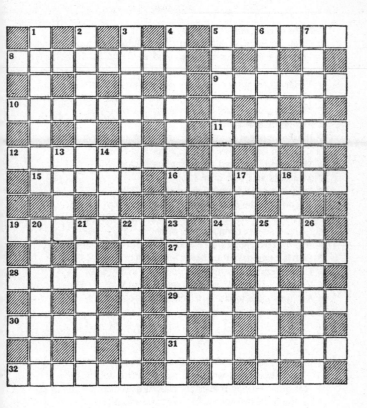

24 Fairy coolers turn up as stable equipment (7)
25 This is useful to those who believe in washing out of sight (3-4)
26 Opportunity for a cross section of the public to express its choice (7)

79

1 Place of retirement for a pluralist? (4-6)

8 Often a terminal trial in short for children (4)

10 These aggressive troops get a good view of a battlefield before action (10)

11 Victim of an early crime in a Belgravian residence (4)

12 To a doctor the main idea is to keep patients out of it! (4)

15 This can be easily spotted in young children (7)

18 Progenitress of pearl (5)

19 It takes a hundred and 11 across to make a spy prototype (5)

20 It should be imitated in war according to Henry V (5)

21 Such forms of bread may circulate smoothly (5)

22 24 across was one once (5)

23 Incurious, free from all signs of debt (5)

24 We doubt if he found South African sunburn too hot! (5)

25 Hall where there is no end to feeding it appears (5)

26 Did she take part on account of her hair? (7)

30 A correspondingly polite address to the company (4)

33 Fish a composer sometimes finishes work with (4)

34 Doing one's job as usual or making a fuss? (8, 2)

35 It should whet your appetite to see what is on it (4)

36 But how's the infant in this northern town? (10)

2 It is not the shape of the ball used here (4)

3 This author could write and do arithmetic too! (5)

4 Not quite making rogues but a good deal more terrifying (5)

5 So the combination shows whom we mean (5)

6 So this must be most painful for all the others (4)

7 May be first-class in thousands yet injure (4)

9 Characteristics that can be irritating (10)

10 A straining thing but it should leave no grounds for complaint (10)

13 It indicates indebtedness, sometimes (10)

14 Descriptive of some wonder-gardens (10)

15 Sicilian seaport (7)

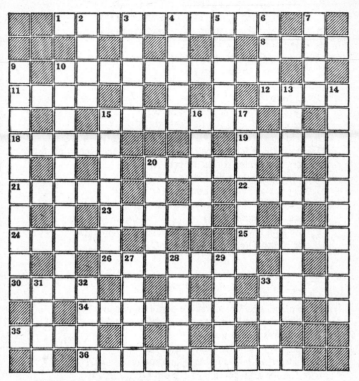

16 Patron saint of a noble race? (5)
17 The predicaments a monkey manages to get into (7)
20 The kind of agreement that requires no signature (5)
27 A sign that something has been left out (5)
28 Harmonize verbally (5)
29 Tendon in a way is new (5)
31 Just a line on 35 across perhaps (4)
32 Almost a huddle of rugger forwards in a film (4)
33 Where so many grease, there must be a twist somewhere (4)

ACROSS

1 Fashion started by one skilled in medicine (5)
4 Might this swan accompany a swan song? (9)
9 Toss the essayist a plant (7)
10 The whole amount is put in the pageant but not very deep (7)
11 Fish, mostly in one spot (4)
12 This creature can make toast (5)
13 £25 horse (4)
16 A workroom that is later modified (7)
17 Distorted Oliver and little Edward (7)
19 An infernal genius is altogether quite slow (7)
22 I am in the money abroad; a little bird may tell you my name (7)
24 A fruity covering for Sir Robert (4)
25 In Surrey it falls a little short of high tea (5)
26 Weapons comfortably arranged (4)
29 Composer of Wye town in self (7)
30 State in the huntress (7)
31 This bend may encourage good fortune (9)
32 One whose charges are often low (5)

DOWN

1 Do actors give sound mature performances in it? (9)
2 What's the result of turning the bed and shaking Alec? (7)
3 Elaine was such a maid (4)
4 A stretch of land or what is used on it (7)
5 Sudden riser puts another interpretation on skill (7)
6 In Europe a kingdom is at the top (4)
7 What some clock-watcher may do to get rid of Bill (4, 3)
8 Disorderly, so naturally starts with a disturbance (5)
14 It's monstrous to take gin at sixes and sevens! (5)
15 This wealthy fellow makes the girls scatter (5)
18 Particularize the pattern consumed (9)
20 Welsh in the home maybe and a help in the theatre (7)
21 You may not belong to this race but to know it helps here (7)
22 Cram a bit of cloth in something rough – it's easily snapped (7)
23 You have never seen such a perfect horseman as he (7)

24 Such an entrance is covered (5)
27 This is drunk but its sap is eaten, oddly enough (4)
28 It's nothing to the noise he is supposed to have made (4)

81

1 'I tied spoon' (anag.) (evidence from the buffet attendant ?) (10)
6 They have many four-in-hand admirers (4)
9 Customs may alter, but it's through them this creeps in (10)
10 See about a thousand, duck (4)
13 Golfer's knockabout, maybe (7)
15 He is all right at heart, and may do a deal for other people (6)
16 This is of no use to the worker who will not do a hand's turn (6)
17 Buying it with the idea of saving money is not a good thing (8, 7)
18 The first letters dispatched didn't arrive, apparently (6)
20 Widespread war-time depression (6)
21 One drug giving some return for effort (7)
22 She is the type any pupil likes to have around (4)
25 The gentle way of London's literary hacks (4, 6)
26 A turn-over of this figure results in a one third loss (4)
27 Un-tasty pig is remaining just where he is (7, 3)

1 Plant honest people don't like to be associated with (4)
2 On the river it is mostly a joke (4)
3 Even in the best set he may have his faults (6)
4 Ambition of a country-minded youngster? (2, 2, 1, 7, 3)
5 Having a mixed gin now (6)
7 Comical pet contrives to tangle things up (10)
8 'We sat there' (anag.) (my this and I?) (10)
11 Being under one may be a promising situation (10)
12 What one makes in 5 down up (10)
13 Bringing up as an occasional equine habit (7)
14 A tough sea-bird reduced to ruin (7)
19 A tower of strength, often, in conflict (6)
20 One may look on the seamy side for it (6)
23 Show grief with a small beginning of pain (4)
24 The best ethics include it, so let it stand (4)

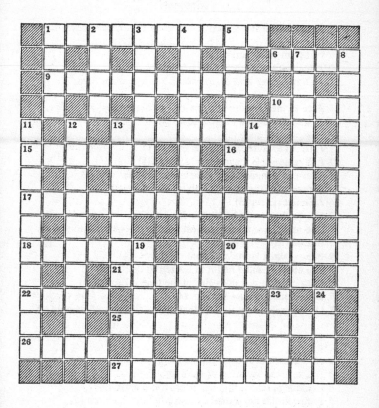

82

1 A broken picture indeed it might be of a broken-down state (11)
9 Anagram of 33 across (4)
10 A handy clue to tracing the criminal (6-5)
11 Man of figures with one of words in a temporary home (4)
14 Interferes with sound awards (7)
18 A sailor nearly over but coming out on top (5)
19 A graduate elected in great haste (5)
20 Uncanonized state (3)
21 A friend to some, a father to many (3)
22 It is responsible for making 10 across (5)
23 They cut themselves but people cut with them too (5)
24 Supporter of the all-round object of a drive (3)
26 A winter runner (3)
27 She displays anger but stands for peace (5)
28 One must have a thorough knowledge of one's subjects to do this well (5)
29 Praise from a latitude without it (7)
33 The alienist should find it in himself to do this (4)
36 With rather a pompous air but the tune is Eton's (11)
37 A studious spot in a hot spot (4)
38 One is made ready for higher things at this type of school (11)

DOWN

2 No longer it provides a get-out (4)
3 Out with this violation of one's rights! (4)
4 Cambridge school that might provide a spree (5)
5 People at this are formally dressed but not energetic (5)
6 An illustrious poet who may have an introduction in music (5)
7 A raider came to be smashed by fellow-feeling (11)
8 It may belong to the kindly waiter (7, 4)
12 He displays refreshment so can give board but no lodging (8-3)
13 Big eel with twisted tail confined and assembled (11)
14 No doubt the team ate it with gusto after the match (4, 3)
15 Cease to be what is cast (3)
16 Human feature hidden in 8 down (3)

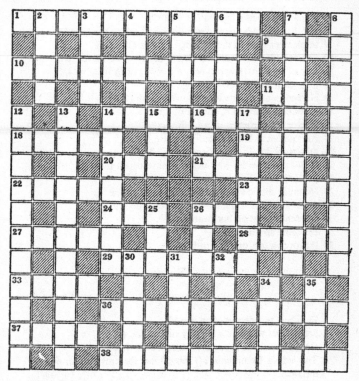

17 To find a little high voice in father may make the Scottish cross (7)

25 Bird always in a bemused state (3)

26 This son is one of four that turns up annually (3)

30 Many back, all dull (5)

31 Til as Blackpool is in the autumn (3, 2)

32 A sound expert at keeping flats up to pitch (5)

34 Droop (4)

35 Does it cling to one's speech? (4)

83

1 Game the Greeks figured out well (7)
5 The freeman who gave common food back to the lady (7)
9 Implement used in the making of shoes (3)
10 Example of feeble running that is mostly fraudulent (7)
11 It is of no signal importance to a motorist in Britain (4, 3)
12 One gains in them by marriage (4)
13 Named in art as one who knows his job (7, 3)
15 All sailors come to it, sooner or later (3, 4)
17 One of the earlier dramatic efforts (7)
19 Alternative to being slated yet again (7)
22 Dog turned colour makes a tasty dish (7)
25 Well-known leader who might turn to couch if set (5, 5)
26 Fastener of military coat or jumper (4)
28 He made music and an antarctic island in one (7)
29 A not unpleasant question of personal ability (7)
30 Consent to put on backwards (3)
31 Do some spotting (7)
32 Put over a fast one in words? (7)

1 Blotched as 1 across often are (7)
2 Set of lines to speak abusively on method (7)
3 One might think it ought to describe the Red Sea! (4)
4 The lady a Communist? Then let her be treated like one of the flock (7)
5 One of Hitler's occupations concerned it (7)
6 It would be difficult to shave oneself without its help (10)
7 Chief example of a topping part with its owner (7)
8 Heart-broken about a man? The usual fiction! (7)
14 'I film lap K.O.' (anag.) (too much to drink defeated the cat?) 4, 2, 4)
16 Not a plant to be glad about (3)
18 Whom the event itself follows (3)
19 Military strings heard on the gramophone (7)

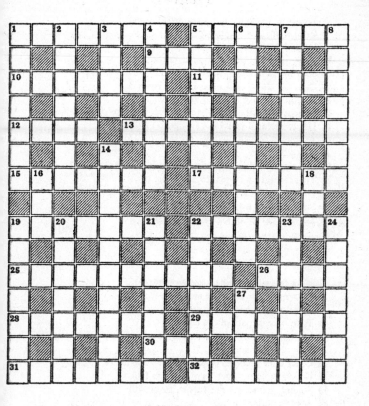

20 The problem of this place has been settled, with initial attempts (7)
21 Short month row to turn away from (7)
22 Undertaking that may turn up as unrefined outside (7)
23 Pity the country where bad rule becomes this (7)
24 With them one can 21 down politely (7)
27 Trimming a letter demon (4)

84

1 This bird seems to be a wide-awake fielder (3-7)
9 Open space in some show (4)
10 Norfolk's gift to the narrow-minded (5, 5)
11 How right it is, although split inside (6)
12 Sporting manoeuvre that is becoming obsolete? (7)
15 One may do it, or it may fly, in a row (7)
16 His work is of growing importance (5)
17 Aggrieved by the come-back of one of those circus fellows (4)
18 Unprofessional backing of a special end (4)
19 Take part in one of those go slow movements? (5)
21 Was (7)
22 Performance that is genuine about most of the city (7)
24 This can turn a boot into a slipper! (6)
27 No epithet for a philanthropist (10)
28 Stick about a way to follow (4)
29 Look bankrupt of expression (5, 5)

2 It's a tempting thing to break a rule (4)
3 No man in them can be reckoned free (6)
4 What's stood in them is reckoned a treat (7)
5 Take note of part of the edition (4)
6 In stealing away from the herd he makes very little noise (7)
7 A symbol of sadness (5, 5)
8 Choir later becomes concerned with the art of speaking (10)
12 Coaching used to get them through (10)
13 Soldier, sailor, but not tinker, tailor (10)
14 There's nothing in medicine if this vessel turns up (5)
15 Not a state of low degree (5)
19 They sound like long drawn out stories, corny too! (7)
20 Fix in amazement with a 29 across? (7)
23 Charge including upsetting of some police (6)
25 There's a ring of virtue about it (4)
26 A catty expression of content (4)

85

1 Such mental weakness does not involve a return to school (6, 9)

9 Is partly but was wholly (7)

10 Lock-holder to be taken on full lock perhaps (7)

11 Scottish church (4)

12 Loud applause, enough to swallow large numbers (5)

13 Where to put the solution (4)

16 Lit up an arrangement of alliance (7)

17 Secure what might be cracked? It secures, anyway (4-3)

18 They may admit taking some punchings (7)

21 Competent headwear to fit (7)

23 Vessels from 30 across (4)

24 The girl is back first to solve the riddle (5)

25 A difficult place on the foreshore (4)

28 Paid artists through to get on (7)

29 Rum and water may become a perfect plague (7)

30 If one does, one is presumably contemptuous, but not a Roman! (5, 2, 4, 4)

DOWN

1 A predecessor of the loud speaker (8-7)

2 It might betray a bird but on reflection the end reveals a cat (7)

3 School's up, set down (4)

4 Will's modifying clause (7)

5 Seal him as an outcast (7)

6 Turn the dial for something Irish (4)

7 Concerning a famous musician (7)

8 Wait upon a double command to take certain steps and when (5, 10)

14 They have turned at the end of 9 across (5)

15 A field of activity to grapple with beheaded (5)

19 Study the round trip in outline (7)

20 This cup is brought out to riders (7)

21 Look out for the fellow, boys, he's a primitive (7)

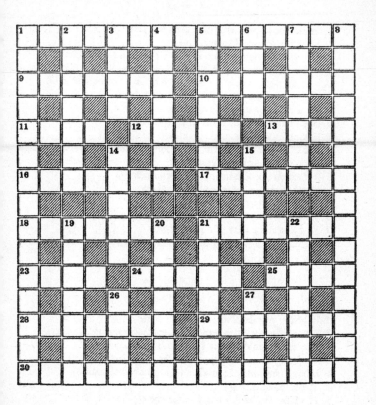

22 Expression of praise about the present epoch is sheer boasting (7)
26 Tear up coupons to study this masterpiece (4)
27 Vessels that sound like luminous bridges (4)

86

1 One needs to pack tightly to start this game (6)
4 Mark the return of spinners (4)
7 It is so small that beheading it may reduce it to one letter (8)
8 Give a sailor the start of it, and an old soldier all of it (6)
10 It is taken for granted to be started again when beheaded (8)
13 Rude to make it? Only if it is to avoid a friend (6)
14 Put a turn in issue and suppressed (3, 4)
15 One should look for them under the ears (6)
18 Having little understanding and less finish (7)
19 One can have nothing but praise for this land (6)
20 Little science or young Edward considered beneath notice (7)
25 In them are people unappreciative of help (6)
26 Mostly a widow, wholly abandoned (8)
27 It's on the house sometimes (6)
28 Stout way to break the law in the beginning (8)
29 To do so is the duty of a retainer (4)
30 Animal with two thirds of elementary education in extremities (6)

1 In giving you a cut he is helping you (6)
2 An addition in letter turns up as evidence of spite (6)
3 The aim is sometimes to speed it to its first part (6)
5 Obviates things that happen for the most part (8)
6 Mixing port with the meal can be reckoned secular (8)
7 The seeds of time (4)
9 The flier who had to hurry at the end (6)
11 The violently insane degrees I can be involved in (7)
12 He suffers from mental inertia, and ends up fat (7)
13 'S.O.S. ride' (anag.) (it's a record!) (7)
16 It may be in a barrel, and shows the animal in the heavy drinker (6)
17 Take a rug for the flier who has taken his last flight (5, 3)
18 The sententious dolt responsible for a telegram about a famous command? (8)

21 What fledglings do in the first part? (6)
22 Just the fellow to give one a hand (6)
23 Row over an insect in Belgium (6)
24 Tots up an old English steer (4)

87

1 A sphere to turn for recorded opinions (6)
4 Interlinked in friendly fashion (3-2-3)
9 In our snuggery we show the most up-to-date (6)
10 The girl who, as Shakespeare might say, has a manner (8)
12 Theatrical blunder, soft enough certainly (5)
13 The world's largest island (9)
15 Desert vermin (3)
16 Greek river mouth (5)
17 One often takes it with 14 down (4)
21 A small letter I think it used to be (4)
24 Unqualified to speak (5)
27 Still in the way, etc. (3)
28 A prison room helps to make it but don't use it for the windows! (9)
31 Blemish of a saint and Scotland's own (5)
32 Repeat manufacture to entertain (8)
33 A country where pipes are indeed deadly (6)
34 This open space made a famous exhibition of itself years ago (4, 4)
35 Do read from it, it's certainly highly thought of (6)

DOWN

1 Genuinely from another language (4, 4)
2 According to established rules there is a possible flaw in it (8)
3 Bird of which a sea-frog is the parent? (9)
5 Land or sea ways (5)
6 A constituent of basic hormones on Olympus (5)
7 An increase in volume into the bargain (2, 4)
8 The first of the fifth (3-3)
11 Take in shrewish form (4)
14 It is used in the late afternoon (3)
18 Where the 'lads' cross the river to see Mrs Gaskell? (9)
19 Terrains rendered capable of rejecting coarse material (8)
20 18 down in fiction (8)

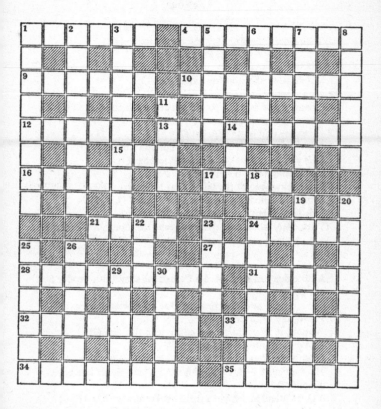

22 Measure supplied by telling (3)
23 The part of 34 across made infamous by Stevenson (4)
25 A little science starts tc burn the surface (6)
26 Does a golfer feel a bit cut up after having done so? (6)
29 Completely exhaust (3, 2)
30 This man and dress are synonymous (5)

ACROSS

1 Greek letter and pole kindling keen interest (7)
5 They may be engaged in mechanical action (4)
9 A maiden's rosy cheek, for example (3, 5, 2, 5)
10 This animal shorn has a pungent smell (4)
11 Wood like a skeleton when beheaded (5)
12 As a measure it is not well finished (4)
15 Gossip about a few if you like, but keep it to yourself (7)
16 One of the weaker vessels? (7)
17 An expression of amusement (7)
19 Gasp about an indecisive finish, but don't be hasty (7)
21 This way so turned can touch the feelings (4)
22 The chief stress has run in (5)
23 In climbing, one of the things that help most (4)
26 Successful outcome of the traveller's tales? (7, 3, 5)
27 This over, there's a demand for punishment! (4)
28 To ponder, but not necessarily to echo the thoughts of others (7)

DOWN

1 A little dog has swallowed a French cat somehow – render first aid (5, 2)
2 Quiet tour in sea leads to a peculiar set of circumstances (5, 9)
3 Part of the Arab Legion (4)
4 Without it most things are easily seen through (7)
5 Bird and ass are royally treated (7)
6 Odd figures that might end up in hospital (4)
7 He may start in a class with others, and finish in a class by himself (7)
8 It turns round in them in a small pool centrally placed (3, 2, 3, 6)
13 Viscous commentary on a sail to windward? (5)
14 Song of a sailor's bag (5)
17 Qualified cover on 3 down (7)
18 Curtailed gardener has become very peeved (7)
19 When this animal loses its head it can hide in a flower (7)
20 It has a bare centre, but might be used to upholster furniture (7)
24 Draw about 50 . . . (4)
25 . . . to help cover this (4)

88

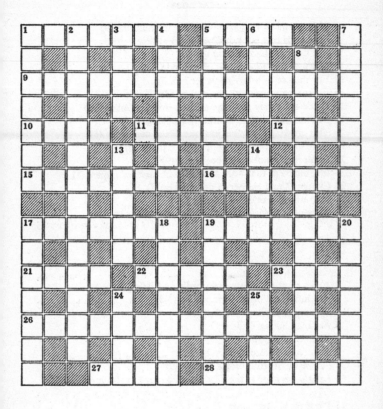

89

1 This luminous ring soon encircles the half-line (9)
9 Arsenal is one but not Chelsea (7)
10 She does, perhaps after a quarrel (5, 2)
11 A severe and unusual word to bind (7)
12 For the use of a bovine writer? (6, 3)
14 Building a vessel with the end on (8)
15 To be on it may give one a down-trodden feeling! (6)
17 In the second place, classically speaking (7)
20 This growing branch is just one of the overheads (6)
23 Here's coal to be hewn – it needs a tie-up (8)
25 Exceedingly bad at the beginning (9)
26 It's imminent that I am a writer with signs of money (7)
27 Charges like a learner in oils, maybe (7)
28 Is it largely a mystery to cook? (7)
29 They utter notes and start a card game (9)

2 Artist climbs in again awkwardly and falls (7)
3 An unfinished drink from a shoe (4-3)
4 Worthy of a shrub like the poet (8)
5 An anag. (anag.) (6)
6 The act of copying (9)
7 Take your choice by this, by Jove! . . . (7)
8 . . . or by St Ernda for a change (9)
13 Peter's associate in the piled up sand may have it on his shoulder (7)
15 Place for a river game (9)
16 Promenade? Yes, and one may along it (9)
18 He was well aware of danger overhead (8)
19 Some more is needed and almost a bottle provides alleviation (7)
21 There's not much value in having a test around four or six (7)
22 Poles keep their distance from it (7)
24 The money we return will be enough for a nut-tree (6)

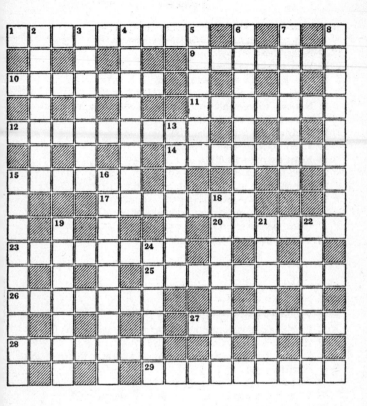

90

1 Little dogs of war? (3-4)

5 This vessel has base associations in America (7)

9 Rather like a mere stain on metal (7)

10 Took a liking to nice change in a crochet (7)

11 Tiny R.A.F. he brought to fighting (2, 3, 4)

12 A work that is the outcome of nothing deep (5)

13 Not only townsmen favour them up North, though they afford calves little protection! (5)

15 Study a thick letter in short (9)

17 Surely not a common colour? (5, 4)

19 Boxes for minerals (5)

22 Land for reverses of fortune (5)

23 Cut off sea to pass into breathless silence (9)

25 Self and scholar get in before to liven things up (7)

26 As a topic of conversation it provides plenty of change for us (7)

27 When this leather is heated crackling is often noticeable (7)

28 Count a girl as abstract (7)

1 The fellow who might tap the hay (7)

2 Problems of this description belong to no single person (7)

3 It was a vicious circle that upset her (5)

4 Some rackets are deliberately designed to beat things of this description (9)

5 Do smokers get it under the eyes? (5)

6 When this affects one it is time to seek relaxation (9)

7 Atrocious result of introducing two of us to common sense (7)

8 Mineral quite commonly used in bridge operations (3, 4)

14 Stealthy approach about drinks as counter propaganda (5, 4)

16 A stormy theatrical scene with this could hardly deliver the goods! (2, 7)

17 Sign that there's a doctor in the house? (3, 4)

18 Revealing a gap caused by boring perhaps (7)

20 Ship of State? (7)

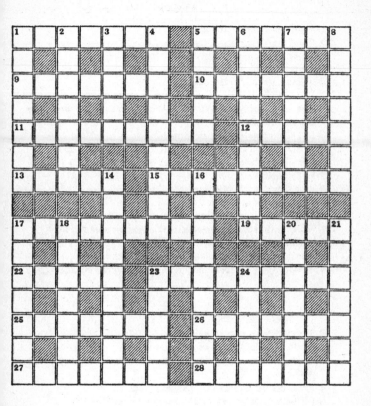

21 Did travellers by stage see more of it than we do? (7)
23 Bright London suburb (5)
24 One kind of unpleasantness I do up for a start (5)

ACROSS

1 A card game for a young Quaker (8)
5 From this comes senna (6)
10 Those to whom so many owed so much in 1940 (2, 3)
11 An early colonist – he was mixed up with the Grail too (7)
12 Balbus carries it in the bus (3)
13 What the Irish have doesn't belong to us (5)
14 One might be given room and board here but it would be criminal to take it (9)
16 Did a run before being airborne (6)
17 Be sly about a disturbed heap and make it presentable (7)
20 Beg for the cane to be changed as one might look (7)
23 Forty winks (3-3)
26 Is this public school connected with a swan census? (9)
29 Rackstraw or the Rover? (5)
30 United briefly as American companies are (3)
31 Many Irishmen are named after this Roman poet . . . (7)
32 . . . who must have worn many these in his time (5)
33 It may be eaten with food and the food with it (6)
34 A shortage in the round may result in temporary blindness (5-3)

DOWN

1 Such language may make one shut up (6)
2 A silk material that flows in Wales first (7)
3 Anglo-Scottish nominal get-together, descriptive of a royal time (9)
4 Describes the old age of a mollusc, no doubt! (7)
6 First-class was first naturally, though unwell (5)
7 An Irish county (5)
8 As trashy as such souvenirs often are (8)
9 Stable fellows who supply their own accommodation (6)
15 One might read it in a glum appearance (3)
18 This describes a part of the world associated with Scott (9)
19 An Ulster graduate could be some support on the way up or down (8)
21 Foreigner of unarmed alliance (3)

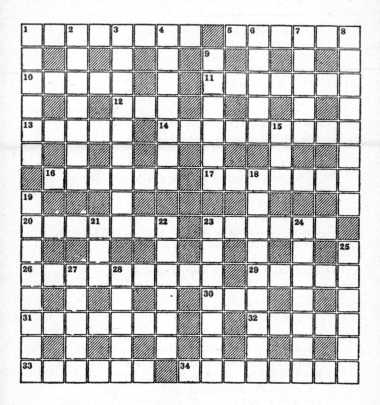

22 Naturally soundly repeated (6)
23 Numbers in coal? How funny! (7)
24 Music to be played by all for example, or in turn, but lively (7)
25 How Patrick would probably ask for silence (6)
27 Danger from a fairy number (5)
28 The numbers to which some dress (5)

92

1 Unfriendly action finally prevailing (6)

4 Little swimmers in a cleft stick (4)

7 At the mercy of current tendencies (8)

8 To be so is at least a feather in one's cap (6)

10 To him nothing is any good (8)

13 Added note to practical charity from the Bible (6)

14 It's nearly all unusually entertaining, so plead for it (7)

15 Not going back after little house material (6)

18 Row back to the vessel for adoration (7)

19 Ask retreating Irish rebels for an African soldier (6)

20 Airman's demand for evidence of approbation (7)

25 Peer's hesitating answer to inquiry as to ownership of robe? (6)

26 Spade ace led to flighty conduct (8)

27 Sufferings on account of those men in the docks? (6)

28 It might be wise to put it on after a strenuous tug-of-war (8)

29 It was surely in evidence when the wicked ogre was destroyed (4)

30 This fellow should work like a Trojan (6)

DOWN

1 Not a very serious affront (6)

2 One would not want one's baby car to have one! (6)

3 If up on a snug home cannot be bettered (6)

5 Appropriate spot from which to make a capital start (4, 4)

6 It's a mule masquerading as ape (8)

7 To the owner of a new car this might mean depression (4)

9 Measured treatment to encourage ailing vocalist . . . (6)

11 . . . . not this note of advice (7)

12 A supporter of the board (7)

13 A region where war made its name ironical (7)

16 Conspicuous portrayal of a parent on canvas (6)

17 Taking the best part of large numbers in a winter sport (8)

18 The arguments he gets into are more likely to be calculated than accidental (8)

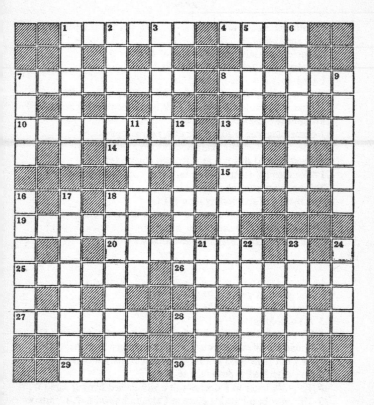

21 Shrewd exclamation in troubled waters (6)
22 It can lower peg after peg and still remain hard headed (6)
23 One must naturally expect him to finish the course behind the others (6)
24 Bent wire contraption that can give some indication of the current (4)

93

ACROSS

6 Both parts of it are heard in church, but it's the softest part of one (5-5)

8 Doctor and sailor and founder of a tribe (4)

9 A man saint from Australasia (9)

11 One does it as the normal thing at 21 across (4)

12 Look about this and you are old – and see nothing (3)

13 Find in it the M.O. stymied? What a shameless business! (9)

16 Expressed after port often (4)

17 Something joined like a bit of a railroad junction (7)

18 Give a number our years and discover bravery (7)

20 Though dead this ran as a Roman church (4)

21 'Team smile' (there's food on these occasions) (anag.) (9)

23 Give this a pen for chance (3)

24 A nymph of resounding fame (4)

25 What a reader may do and a traveller hopes to get filled (5-4)

29 Scottish island, except one letter (4)

30 An old measure beginning oval-shaped (10)

DOWN

1 The smallest particle to change with (4)

2 Upshot of a shot at the table, maybe (4)

3 An oilseed (4)

4 It's glue that is responsible for this most unpleasant result (7)

5 Found on rifle ranges due to vehicles going across them? (10)

7 Ann not gay? She must be at the end of her tether (5-4)

8 Poe described a descent into it (9)

10 To put a letter in a doctor's title will indeed honour him (3)

13 This may be a meeting-place in Calcutta known to P.T. instructors (6, 4)

14 Artists in Cornwall admire this small animal refuge (9)

15 Separate into elements (9)

19 Scarcely with timidity but little more than scarcely (7)

22 Initially a bugbear to South African diamond producers (3)

26 One of several one must know to be well-informed (4)

27 An American State (4)

28 To break some flints might precede the sack for a traveller (4)

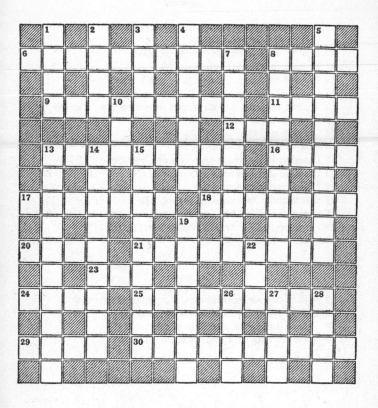

94

1 'Port be fine' (anag.) (but many think this is better) (4, 2, 4)
9 To this was once as well (4)
10 Law we liked to be easily influenced (4-6)
11 By no means robust in business (6)
12 Her suit has become rather like a penitent's shirt (7)
15 Not wholly inapplicable to the floating voter (7)
16 It could suggest art to some, and comfort to a number (5)
17 A hindrance to vision . . . (4)
18 . . . that may this with the sun (4)
19 Rest with shelter included (5)
21 Descriptive of a clock that goes one over the eight? (4-3)
22 Excellent in colour and nicely polished (7)
24 If we could substitute a liking for it quarrels would cease (6)
27 Satisfactorily explained, though C.I.D. due late for it (10)
28 It may sound good to a hungry man . . . (4)
29 . . . hoping that it heralds what is inwardly this (10)

2 A good observer uses his eyes, and not these things (4)
3 They are all right in numbers for marks (6)
4 There's destiny about the rig of this vessel (7)
5 We don't take such measures these days (4)
6 More than liberal when used of a . . . (7)
7 . . . this (10)
8 Give us malt diet in form to be stirred up (10)
12 Hand me gags in the shape of food (3, 3, 4)
13 A kind of 24 across dispatched me to tear about (10)
14 Mostly noble betimes (5)
15 He starts favourite, in any event (5)
19 Their work with logs is mathematically exact (7)
20 Allows its end under the waves! (7)
23 In sporting association my result is of shocking repute (6)
25 One might get a laugh out of curtailing this vessel (4)
26 The answer is observed to be seven minus five (4)

94

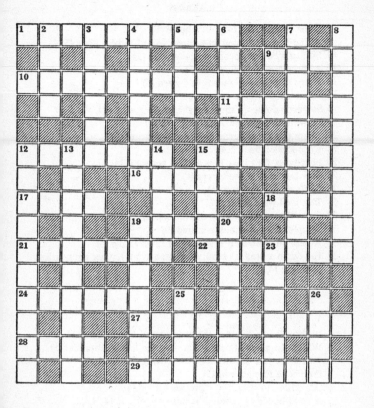

193

95

1 Some perceive the lady on a horse (9)
9 At the end of training an engineer joined to be a diver (5)
10 Fish to a body of people is quite plain (9)
11 A sheep swallows numbers (5)
12 Thane disperses to a place in Cymru (5)
14 Suitable material to creep around in (5)
16 Someone doing up shoes maybe, making a row (4)
19 Draw back from the engineers' area (7)
21 Steam this is colloquial and has no pictures (5)
22 Unconcealed duck beside the green (5)
23 First born, they have eyes and do not see (7)
24 Sore but back in the Circus (4)
25 One's rate of progress (5)
27 This land was for hire? (5)
30 Get a fish or turn some achievement (5)
32 Sample not so much, it's insipid (9)
33 A baboon often seen at Aldershot for example (5)
34 Far down a piece of land; hoping to avoid having boundaries, of course (4, 5)

2 It's best if I go between the Spanish and French turn (5)
3 What's the game? Pussy swallowing the fellow! Swindle! (5)
4 This artist can do without little Elizabeth's head (4)
5 Present of foreign iron (5)
6 Something to open for a precious stone (5)
7 A good boiled egg should be most opportune (4-5)
8 Consumed with anger at first, moderate now (9)
13 The bird from the end of 1 across (5)
14 Precious stone wanted from case yet to be solved (4-3)
15 In French the sailor came first being authorized (7)
17 A smuggler would surely advocate this sort of business (4, 5)
18 A colloquial equivalent of the vernacular (9)
20 It's up to the song-writer (5)
25 The lady will shortly become explosive! (5)

26 To avoid the girl takes a little detour (5)
28 Stew from Islam (5)
29 Support, needed in idea-selling (5)
31 . (4)

96

1 For a blue ribbon sporter in trunks these might hold soft drinks! (7)

5 A familiar settler in the home (4)

9 Bill of fruit came to a crown (7, 2, 6)

10 This king is engaged in mental exercise (4)

11 Frequent article in quest (5)

12 A boss among rank nobodies (4)

15 Nowadays three or four lanes may go to make up one (7)

16 It gives pain to the listener (7)

17 All is for some who die, and most for some who dye (7)

19 A course crossed by many who holiday abroad (7)

21 Some of them are tightened by braces (4)

22 Puts nothing into pawn, vulgarly speaking (5)

23 Portent from endings of beginnings (4)

26 Court asset that makes for satisfied customers (8, 7)

27 Wager a second letter (4)

28 Many toiled for reward, and were the wiser for it (7)

DOWN

1 Put up a snare to irritate and charm (7)

2 Reckoning to enlist the hearers' sympathy? (7, 3, 4)

3 If it's a bully one, it is titled (4)

4 Sounds descriptive of a fine warm spell, but is short (7)

5 Instinctive action against strikers (7)

6 Give Noah this island for his creation (4)

7 How to shake a thousand in three times (7)

8 Not quite free from terms of contract (2, 3, 9)

13 A roundabout companion? (5)

14 Vision of a lot of paper? (5)

17 He has no special rank (7)

18 Morning attraction on a coronation vessel (7)

19 He might have a brief interest in the 5 down (7)

20 It can produce crops in the open, but is seen differently in cover (7)

24 One thing China would hate to lose (4)

25 Ventilate a reversal vocally (4)

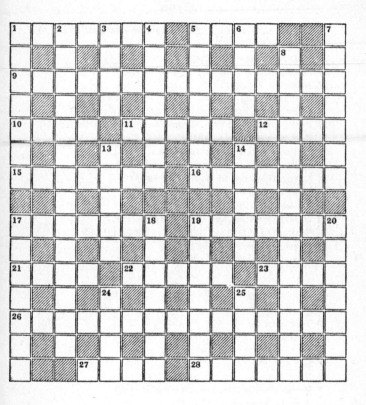

97

1 Charred feathers as the result of a severe conflagration? (5, 4)
9 A kind of scout (5)
10 It takes a master-man to create such weapons (9)
11 Not the sort of shaft a miner would use (5)
12 A foreign soldier (5)
14 A musically soft row that is only a bit of mischief (5)
16 Sounds mean but it may be of a generous character (4)
19 Broke the old gate and indulged in reprehensible feelings (7)
21 Rather contemptuous language (5)
22 Just over a yard is the extent of this island (5)
23 Fencing thrust to a learner makes a bird of prey (7)
24 Information from all main directions (4)
25 Bring on food to start the game (5)
27 It takes more than ages to wipe out (5)
30 Nautically vertical and mostly a vegetable (5)
32 'Bristol M.O.' (anag.) (rather hot-headed?) (9)
33 A thing in a way but obscure (5)
34 Inexpensive players in London (9)

DOWN

2 Tear apart (5)
3 Heathen, short of one male, as found in Wales (5)
4 He is responsible for the deed (4)
5 See 6 down.
6 With 5 down. A mole, perhaps (5-5)
7 It might be rivetable but can be avoided (9)
8 A bird's home on board (5-4)
13 Look for it in mining other metals (5)
14 One in a pillar may break new ground (7)
15 One or two paragraphs only, maybe, to make it clear (7)
17 Tropical fruits often found in English lawns (9)
18 Be acquainted with a shelf that provides learning (9)
20 Led up first to dig (5)
25 This fish is not necessarily found in icy waters (5)
26 A few cut into the weed (5)

28 This Pierre in France was a revolutionary character (5)
29 What 5 down becomes at low temperatures (5)
31 Many have had their spirits lightened by it (4)

ACROSS

1 The next big bridge they will build in Scotland? (5)
4 Pet visitor to London, known in the nursery (5, 3)
10 Let the common run come to cringe (7)
11 Suffering from shortage of time as in the rearrangement (2, 5)
12 It may grow in the garden or be scattered there (4)
13 Pigment of a headless river (5)
14 Strike or attend when divided (4)
17 Consecutive numbers associated with confusion (5, 3, 6)
19 Powers which don't seem to get together (8, 6)
22 Pre-eminent vault (4)
23 Burning to go but interrupted by broken law (5)
24 A sordine (4)
27 This surgery has often put a new face on hospital work (7)
28 Cropped like a rabbit (7)
29 Italian island dance? (8)
30 Made more comfortable but with short December death came (5)

DOWN

1 If at last he met sudden death, he would half expect it (8)
2 Completely bewilder so to speak (7)
3 A fish of the cod family (4)
5 Meat for us all? Much may turn on it (9, 5)
6 One may find a school without numbers here (4)
7 With over a hundred to the back it can hold a lot of liquid (7)
8 A small noise with a very small heart (5)
9 This inexactitude is a polite lie (14)
15 Like a Scot it denotes a foreigner (5)
16 A French military aircraft (5)
18 Went up as a hundred finished (8)
20 This would light only part of the family circle presumably (3-4)
21 Associated with curtain lectures, they are warm to drink too (7)
22 Snake numbers, good to eat (5)
25 The case of one who mends? (4)
26 Competent to upset a bale (4)

ACROSS

5 Look for a letter to cut open (6)

8 Ward as a disadvantage (8)

9 Peter and Miss Spenlow who had a box (7)

10 Poor S——, the track ruined him (5)

11 Not needing glasses the bird looked like this (5-4)

13 They are not paid by the A.A.A. but they may pay the A.A. (8)

14 French city a bit typical of the precision required (6)

17 Bacon's relatively poor actor (3)

19 What is inside this may well cause a crack-up (3)

20 Play may provide such a run, though it's not a hit (3-3)

23 Corsican takes game, love fifty and a bad one (8)

26 Bird that makes a hundred rant about a broken moor (9)

28 Savoury bit of ice cream to follow 12 down (5)

29 This retort may well contain acid of a kind (7)

30 A creator of perfection (8)

31 Gift of drink in an explosive situation (6)

DOWN

1 Port does as it is shaken (6)

2 Russian infuser of China, perhaps (7)

3 A famous surgeon and a hard biscuit (9)

4 A game recorder whose heart is in the right place (6)

5 A poet on the heather and fishy too (8)

6 Muddle caused by putting twopence in the liquor (5)

7 The commanding officer is naturally first in this vessel (8)

12 Must change the health resort – it's poisonous (3)

15 If this is bliss then we are all in some degree happy (9)

16 A Spaniard takes it a miss (8)

18 This is a cert. for a student who is sick (8)

21 Refreshing place in the north (3)

22 Emotion released by 9 across (7)

24 Dress at the top and change the form of procedure (6)

25 Mark the French up and get some money (6)

27 Love some reformed animal here (5)

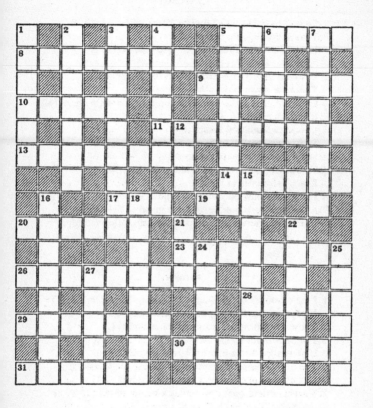

100

1 'Is read to pals' (anag.) (poetry lovers, of course) (8, 4)
9 The Albert Hall, for example? (7)
10 It could be cruel about a doctor, to break up so (7)
11 Stick to it for a club? (4)
12 The pied variety was attractive to the young (5)
13 To turn it down is not a bright idea (4)
16 Something laid by to help bring up the children, perhaps (4-3)
17 It's mother, not it! (7)
18 Checks two military bodies (7)
21 Sand not disturbed to have underfoot (5, 2)
23 Some grow it to make money (4)
24 To be incorrect in my set is altogether gay (5)
25 Reach for bumps in it? (4)
28 It is money now only in slang (7)
29 A feeling that is doubly unfortunate when heartless (3, 4)
30 One may admire their rich panoply before they fall (6, 6)

1 Very devout about half-term, but altogether deplorable (7)
2 If you frequent this you may be slipping! (4)
3 Those who cheat in it can win hands down! (7)
4 Fish that shoot up (7)
5 If you called him a smart fellow you would be quite a lot out (4)
6 The day clever people turn up to have a good wash? (7)
7 Prober in smoke reveals a breach of faith (6, 7)
8 To what extent one uses them is a matter of taste (6, 3, 4)
14 Sporting the second half of 30 across (5)
15 If it were heartless, the miner and not the diver would find it (5)
19 Headwear possibly noticeable in a girl, and in her young man (7)
20 Headwear a marginal comment is shortly on (7)
21 In delivering it one may hope for some net return (7)
22 The last word on parade (7)
26 Peruse without allowing for final directions (4)
27 He is little less than a bondman (4)

SOLUTIONS

No. 1

ACROSS. – 1, Commandant; 6, Boom; 9, Materially; 10, Feat; 13, Messiah; 15, Orison; 16, Hostel; 17, Negative results; 18, Averse; 20, Anselm; 21, Evening; 22, Ivor; 25, Inebriated; 26, Some; 27, Wet weather.

DOWN. – 1, Camp; 2, Mite; 3, Airmen; 4, Draws the long bow; 5, Nullah; 7, Overtilted; 8, Mettlesome; 11, Boundaries; 12, Single room; 13, Mortise; 14, Housing; 19, Evince; 20, Angina; 23, Itch; 24, Oder.

No. 2

ACROSS. – 1, Mitigation; 6, Kale; 10, Wedge; 11, Red-handed; 12, Sybarite; 13, Resin; 15, Pressed; 17, Dog-rose; 19, Carrots; 21, Silence; 22, Argot; 24, Long life; 27, Indignant; 28, Thorn; 29, Yoyo; 30, Near the top.

DOWN. – 1, Mews; 2, Teddy bear; 3, Greta; 4, Tarried; 5, Old head; 7, Andes; 8, Endangered; 9, Madrigal; 14, Speciality; 16, Shortage; 18, Own effort; 20, Salvage; 21, Senator; 23, Giddy; 25, Latch; 26, Snap.

No. 3

ACROSS. – 1, Palindromes; 8, Pips; 9, Solent; 12, Cold; 13, Area; 14, Egg; 15, Overseer; 17, Impede; 18, Lessees; 20, Ignites; 24, Object; 26, Fandango; 28, Oar; 29, Ribs; 31, Sere; 32, Static; 33, Spar; 34, Studentship.

DOWN. – 2, Avid; 3, Insane; 4, Dusters; 5, Obliging; 6, Edna; 7, School board; 8, Pliers; 10, True; 11, Baker's dozen; 16, See; 19, Extorted; 21, Nod; 22, Tender; 23, African; 25, Jobs; 27, Nurses; 30, Stet; 31, Sari.

No. 4

ACROSS. – 1, On the left; 9, Sneeze; 10, Date stamp; 11, Rescue; 12, Illegible; 13, Scarab; 17, Who; 19, Convenient place; 20, Tie; 21, Pewter; 25, Black eyes; 26, Gutter; 27, Dominions; 28, Air ace; 29, Assenting.

DOWN. – 2, Nearly; 3, Heeded; 4, Lithia; 5, Family heirlooms; 6, Intercept; 7, Mercurial; 8, Resembled; 14, Scapegoat; 15, Snow-storm; 16, Deference; 17, Wit; 18, One; 22, Active; 23, Depict; 24, Vernon.

No. 5

ACROSS. – 1, Out of bounds; 8, Stet; 9, Talk to; 12, Oslo; 13, Alti; 14, Raw; 15, Napoleon; 17, Far and; 18, In proof; 20, Flemish; 24, Sonata; 26, Long-stop; 28, Pea; 29, Ursa; 31, Oral; 32, Tweeds; 33, Loan; 34, Hypertrophy.

Down. – 2, Unto; 3, Obtuse; 4, By turns; 5, Unlawful; 6, Data; 7, Connoisseur; 8, Slip up; 10, Olga; 11, Gild the pill; 16, Leo; 19, Of a piece; 21, Egg; 22, Intern; 23, Plays at; 25, Nest; 27, Niello; 30, Away; 31, Oath.

No. 6

Across. – 5, Mobile; 8, Breakage; 9, Shroud; 10, Feel well; 11, Eulogy; 12, Milk-powder; 15, Beery; 16, Strode; 19, Gramme; 24, Teeth; 27, Run the show; 28, Factor; 29, The dumps; 30, Impact; 31, Cut no ice; 32, Anselm.

Down. – 1, True rib; 2, Catlike; 3, Page-boy; 4, Seclude; 5, Misters; 6, Burglar; 7, Lounged; 13, Leda; 14, Prom; 17, Tree; 18, Unth; 20, Roadmen; 21, My trade; 22, Erratum; 23, Unstuck; 24, Threats; 25, Escudos; 26, Hospice.

No. 7

Across. – 1, Flapjacks; 6, Habit; 9, Novelette; 10, Ruler; 11, Rum; 12, Sally Lunn; 15, Irate; 16, Pacts; 19, Drama; 21, Opt; 22, Use; 23, Verdi; 24, Elgar; 26, Baton; 27, Courtyard; 31, Two; 32, Inure; 33, Newmarket; 35, Essen; 36, Serenades.

Down. – 1, Finis; 2, Anvil; 3, Jelly; 4, Cot; 5, Stern; 6, Hermitage; 7, Billabong; 8, Tormentor; 13, Let; 14, Under; 16, Plumb-line; 17, Chestnuts; 18, Seventeen; 20, Adieu; 25, Lay; 27, Cones; 28, Twain; 29, Asked; 30, Dates; 34, War.

No. 8

Across. – 1, Dower house; 6, Epic; 9, Faint heart; 10, Barm; 13, Snooker; 15, Stalag; 16, Duenna; 17, Naboth's vineyard; 18, Errors; 20, Euston; 21, Easiest; 22, Duet; 25, Semicircle; 26, Dolt; 27, Open mouths.

Down. – 1, Daft; 2, Whig; 3, Rating; 4, One's own volition; 5, Screed; 7, Plain facts; 8, Commanding; 11, As intended; 12, Camberwell; 13, Saltire; 14, Rule out; 19, Save up; 20, Eskimo; 23, Scot; 24 News.

No. 9

Across. – 1, Unprepared; 8, Racial; 9, Paper money; 10, Immune; 11, Contention; 12, Gutter; 13, Menu; 15, Dwindle; 19, Oppress; 21, Owed; 22, Stanza; 25, Duck-boards; 27, Ordeal; 28, Increasing; 29, Nelson; 30, Effortless.

Down. – 1, Unpacked; 2, Piping; 3, Earner; 4, About; 5, Drying up; 6, Scimitar; 7, Painters; 13, Mew; 14, Nod; 16, Water-hen; 17, Nonsense; 18, Load-line; 20, Sausages; 23, Cobalt; 24, Praise; 26, Karoo.

No. 10

Across. – 1, Hopeful; 5, Gambles; 9, Already; 10, Shadoof; 11, Try it on; 15, Enlists; 19, Agate; 21, Unpack; 22, Walled; 23, Toots; 24, Wether; 25, Oracle; 26, Eaton; 29, Ushered; 32, Ogreish; 36, Leering; 37, Leasing; 38, Tasters; 39, Spender.

Down. – 1, Heart; 2, Party; 3, Feast; 4, Laying; 5, Gasket; 6, Miaul; 7, Loops; 8, Sifts; 12, Runners; 13, Ivanhoe; 14, Oak-tree; 16, New song; 17, Ill-fame; 18, Trellis; 20, Afoot; 27, Adages; 28, Oodles; 29, Unlit; 30, Heels; 31, Rhine; 33, Reade; 34, Ivied; 35, Hagar.

No. 11

Across. – 1, Madeira; 5, Ouse; 9, Coming to the fore; 10, Also; 11, Given; 12, Etch; 15, En masse; 16, Tugboat; 17, Coquets; 19, Pleased; 21, Alas; 22, Fanny; 23, Inks; 26, Pressed for space; 27, Edgy; 28, Aroused.

Down. – 1, Macrame; 2, Demisemiquaver; 3, Inns; 4, Astride; 5, On the QT; 6, Sued; 7, Freshet; 8, Month of Sundays; 13, Askew; 14, Agree; 17, Crampon; 18, Standby; 19, Pandora; 20, Distend; 24, Used; 25, Oslo.

No. 12

Across. – 1, Blasted; 5, Chariot; 9, In panic; 10, Ungodly; 11, Air; 12, Flaccid; 16, Cartage; 20, Delhi; 22, Snooze; 23, Maitre; 24, Angel; 25, D'hotel; 26, Equine; 27, Lends; 30, Apteryx; 33, Essenes; 37, Elm; 38, Flipper; 39, Atomize; 40, Lathers; 41, Ditched.

Down. – 1, Brief; 2, Alpha; 3, Tonic; 4, Decade; 5, Church; 6, Anger; 7, India; 8, Thyme; 13, Long hop; 14, Chortle; 15, Ideally; 17, Aimless; 18, Tribune; 19, Gironde; 21, Logan; 28, Exerts; 29, Demand; 30, Awful; 31, Taint; 32, Rupee; 34, Sport; 35, Neigh; 36, Speed.

No. 13

Across. – 5, Hamper; 8, Carapace; 9, Ranker; 10, Graceful; 11, Adenoids; 12, Said; 14, Err; 15, Wyvern; 16, Elements; 19, Turned up; 23, Clinch; 26, Ash; 27, Nero; 28, Travesty; 29, Rifleman; 31, Callao; 32, Leinster; 33, Byword.

Down. – 1, Fairway; 2, Cascade; 3, Calf; 4, Declare; 5, Horse-leech; 6, Manhole; 7, Emend it; 12, Swot; 13, Ivor; 14, End discord; 17, None; 18, Soho; 20, Unready; 21, Novello; 22, Pay-roll; 24, Incense; 25, Creases; 30, Flip.

No. 14

Across. – 1, New policy; 9, Hosier; 10, South wind; 11, Static; 12, Five years; 13, Astral; 17, Ate; 19, Artful customers; 20, Elk; 21, Twinge; 25, Stock-whip; 26, Greens; 27, Contagion; 28, Truism; 29, Essential.

Down. – 2, Exotic; 3, Pother; 4, Lawyer; 5, Congratulations; 6, Contusion; 7, Disturbed; 8, Priceless; 14, Castigate; 15, Strike out; 16, Dungeness; 17, Ace; 18, Esk; 22, Scathe; 23, Dwight; 24, Mimosa.

No. 15

Across. – 1, Mangosteen, 9, Thee; 10, Great wheel; 11, Lets go; 12, Rutty; 15, Ethyl; 18, Ruler, 19, Outrage; 20, Topsy; 21, Swiss; 22, Askance; 23, Until; 24, Tagus; 26, Snort; 29, Iceman; 31, Anglicized; 32, Said; 33, Kingfisher.

Down. – 2, Acre; 3, Go away; 4, Sewer; 5, Exeat; 6, Nefly; 7, Chiselling; 8, Bed of roses; 13, Untaken; 14, Trainer; 15, Enthusiasm; 16, Hypothetic; 17, Loyal; 18, Reset; 25, Allies; 26, Snark; 27, Organ; 28, Thief; 30, Mere.

No. 16

Across. – 1, Hammock; 4, Chaotic; 9, Countermand; 11, Dear; 12, Sect; 13, Platter; 15, Ladies; 16, Dealer; 17, Ada; 19, Repair; 20, Papers; 22, Tot; 25, Shoots; 27, Clutch; 28, Several; 29, Reed; 31, Dots; 32, Rapscallion; 33, Helping; 34, Essence.

Down. – 1, Holdall; 2, Moor; 3, Canals; 5, Humped; 6, Owns; 7, Costers; 8, Melted; 9, Candle-power; 10, Declaration; 13, Pedants; 14, Redpoll; 17, Art; 18, Apt; 21, Ostrich; 23, Operas; 24, Thistle; 26, Season; 27, Cables; 30, Damp; 31, Dole.

No. 17

Across. – 1, Hawthorn; 5, Ack-ack; 9, Regicide; 10, Comely; 12, Neats-foot; 14, Knout; 15, Taw; 16, Potato; 18, Ibsen; 21, Laird, 22, Sanded; 24, Ego; 27, Fakir; 28, Handshake; 31, Ushers; 32, Toboggan; 33, Siwash; 34, Headgear.

Down. – 1, Hiring; 2, Wigwam; 3, Hocks; 4, Radio; 6, Clockwise; 7, Ale-house; 8, Keystone; 11, Otto; 13, Fit; 17, Order arms; 19, All fours; 20, Kickshaw; 22, Soho; 23, Dud; 25, Wangle; 26, Jenner; 29, Noose; 30, Stood.

No. 18

Across. – 1, Circus ring; 9, Peri; 10, Good artist; 11, Extant; 12, Momus; 15, Bully; 18, Filer; 19, Asperse; 20, Aztec; 21, Verdi; 22, Hostile; 23, Knout; 24, Rayon; 26, Edges; 29, Rarity; 31, On the slate; 32, Amps; 33, Sand-storms.

Down. – 2, Idol; 3, Cudgel; 4, Scrum; 5, Idiom; 6, Gates; 7, Metallurgy; 8, Distortion; 13, Opposed; 14, Upraise; 15, Black bread; 16, Lithograph; 17, Yacht; 18, Fever; 25, Apollo; 26, Eyots; 27, Get on; 28, Seeds; 30, Atom.

No. 19

Across. – 1, Ruffled; 5, Pith; 9, Magazine stories; 10, Awry; 11, Often; 12, Chic; 15, Trooper; 16, Sea-wall; 17, Cossack; 19, Cambric; 21, Oxen; 22, Medal; 23, Oboe; 26, Packet of gaspers; 27, Flat; 28, Strayed.

Down. – 1, Remnant; 2, Figure of speech; 3, Laze; 4, Done for; 5, Pastels; 6, Tool; 7, Musical; 8, Highway robbery; 13, Sprat; 14, Halma; 17, Chopper; 18, Keep out; 19, Coal-gas; 20, Creased; 24, Peel; 25, Yser.

No. 20

Across. – 1, Relationship; 8, Paradox; 9, Tumbler; 12, Cubs; 13, Brunt; 14, Carp; 17, Attache; 18, Rosetta; 19, Aground; 22, Know-how; 24, Else; 25, Warns; 26, Wren; 29, Throats; 31, Cordial; 32, Maiden speech.

Down. – 1, Rarebit; 2, Lady; 3, Tax-free; 4, Oftener; 5, Same; 6, Poe; 7, Special agent; 10, Leant; 11, Rip van Winkle; 15, Scout; 16, Ascot; 20, Riser; 21, Drags on; 22, Kingcup; 23, Harwich; 27, Card; 28, Urge; 30, Hum.

No. 21

Across. – 1, Beefeater; 6, Brand; 9, Charger; 10, Deserts; 11, Note; 12, Gaffe; 13, Once; 16, Mad hatter; 18, Sheba; 19, Sides; 21, Bando-lero; 23, Lees; 24, Clamp; 26, Spot; 30, Tempest; 31, Sporran; 32, Error; 33, Dark horse.

Down. – 1, Bacon; 2, Enacted; 3, Ergo; 4, Terra; 5, Rod of iron; 6, Bass; 7, Arrange; 8, Desperado; 14, Passe; 15, Ascot; 16, Mistletoe; 17, Tabulated; 20, Dreamer; 22, Emperor; 25, Miser; 27, Tense; 28, Peer; 29, Moth.

No. 22

Across. – 8, Depreciate; 9, Lava; 10, Buckingham; 11, Mute; 12, Spring song; 17, Braid; 20, Nick; 21, Fags; 23, Earth; 24, Red herring; 30, Mice; 31, Monumental; 32, Nuts; 33, Little slam.

Down. – 1, Venus; 2, Broken in; 3, Scones; 4, Washer; 5, Vermin; 6, Caruso; 7, Bad egg; 13, Poker; 14, In fun; 15, Gage; 16, Next; 18, Robe; 19, Dice; 22, Sameness; 24, Romany; 25, Ducats; 26, Ramble; 27, Innate; 28, Gamble; 29, Satan.

No. 23

Across. – 1, Short of money; 9, Octagon; 10, Samaria; 11, Nine; 12, Agony; 13, Scud; 16, Excerpt; 17, Tonneau; 18, Postman; 21, Bulwark; 23, Leak; 24, Twice; 25, Boot; 28, Candles; 29, Learner; 30, Prevaricated.

Down. – 1, Satanic; 2, Orgy; 3, Tonight; 4, Fastnet; 5, O.H.M.S.; 6, Ear-ache; 7, Mounted police; 8, Hard luck story; 14, Tramp; 15, Knell; 19, Spanner; 20, No wiser; 21, Bucolic; 22, Adorned; 26, Slav; 27, Cast.

No. 24

Across. – 1, Stalingrad; 9, Otto; 10, Swordsmith; 11, Octavo; 12, Bestial; 15, Seringa; 16, Gusty; 17, Sets; 18, Semi; 19, Sides; 21, Sus-pend; 22, Pomatum; 24, Lay off; 27, Fatherless; 28, Erne; 29, Daily dozen.

Down. – 2, Town; 3, Lariat; 4, Nosebag; 5, Rain; 6, Dahomey; 7, Attainment; 8, Honorarium; 12, Best seller; 13, Satisfying; 14, Lucid; 15, Steep; 19, Snuffed; 20, Sorcery; 23, Apollo; 25, Etui; 26, Isle.

No. 25

Across. – 8, Winchester; 9, Felt; 10, Stupendous; 11, Dean; 12, Pagan rites; 17, Which; 20, Soap; 21, Mood; 23, Dunes; 24, Poppy seeds; 30, Tort; 31, Timber-wolf; 32, Suet; 33, Rosy cheeks.

Down. – 1, Wilts; 2, Sceptics; 3, Sewn up; 4, Strong; 5, Prison; 6, Defeat; 7, Stunts; 13, Apple; 14, Armed; 15, Rood; 16, Ease; 18, Halo; 19, Holy; 22, Duckweed; 24, Potash; 25, Parley; 26, Satire; 27, Enmesh; 28, Speech; 29, Slake.

No. 26

ACROSS. – 5, Tackle; 8, Thick ear; 9, Wooing; 10, Brooding; 11, Archer; 12, Counted out; 15, Titan; 16, Honest; 19, Retina; 24, Heart; 27, Ginger snap; 28, Supple; 29, Tethered; 30, Gillie; 31, Abetting; 32, Recess.

DOWN. – 1, Chariot; 2, Account; 3, Denizen; 4, Dragoon; 5, Towpath; 6, Coon-can; 7, Lancers; 13, Uist; 14, Tarn; 17, Over; 18, Earn; 20, Elusive; 21, Impulse; 22, Ageless; 23, Instead; 24, Heather; 25, Assents; 26, Taverns.

No. 27

ACROSS. – 1, Cremona; 8, Back-end; 9, Monocle; 10, Ananias; 11, Steeple; 14, Assort; 18, Dense; 20, Insert; 22, Tip-top; 23, Ewers; 25, No side; 28, Tuesday; 29, Outsize; 32, Amateur; 33, Caviare; 34, History.

DOWN. – 1, Commission; 2, Eons; 3, Orcs; 4, Averted; 5, Mainmast; 6, Skunks; 7, Unfair; 12, Eases; 13, Pared, 15, Seize; 16, Oxted; 17, Topsy-turvy; 19, Ear; 21, Tweezers; 24, Stomach; 26, Ocular; 27, Instil; 30, Pass; 31, Nero.

No. 28

ACROSS. – 1, Pickpocket; 8, Heroin; 9, Importance; 10, Elated; 11, Roehampton; 12, Ethics; 13, Poem; 15, Enclose; 19, Lyddite; 21, Opal; 22, Winner; 25, Contradict; 27, Parsee; 28, Rising tide, 29, Scheme; 30, Rudderless.

DOWN. – 1, Primrose; 2, Copper; 3, Portal; 4, Clasp; 5, The enemy; 6, Preached; 7, Civet-cat; 13, Pep; 14, Ell; 16, Nuisance; 17, Landseer; 18, Sorcerer; 20, Editress; 23, Manger; 24, Virile; 26, Third.

No. 29

ACROSS. – 1, Catastrophe; 7, Spanish; 8, Impeach; 10, Pain; 11, Codex; 13, User; 15, Led; 17, Rheims; 19, Persia; 20, Penally; 21, Impale; 23, Yelped; 25, Sun; 27, Ills; 28, Queue; 29, Aria; 32, Spilled; 33, Rampant; 34, Never say die.

DOWN. – 1, Cyanide; 2, Tail; 3, School; 4, Ruined; 5, Papa; 6, Elapses; 7, Superficies; 9, Hard and fast; 12, Devalue; 14, Ample; 16, Keyes; 18, See; 19, Ply; 22, Pillion; 24, Partake; 25, Sunder; 26, Nutria; 30, Slav; 31, Amid.

No. 30

ACROSS. – 5, Walrus; 8, Carolina; 9, Robust; 10, Shopping; 11, Annual; 12, Passport; 15, Titan; 16, Extended; 19, Oak chest; 24, Paddy; 27, Wormwood; 28, Gossip; 29, Ruminant; 30, Finite; 31, Extolled; 32, Verges.

DOWN. – 1, Bath-mat; 2, Compost; 3, Pig-iron; 4, Margate; 5, Warrant; 6, Lebanon; 7, Upstage; 13, Sink; 14, Path; 17, Edam; 18, Dodo; 20, Aconite; 21, Casting; 22, Express; 23, Twirled; 24, Promote; 25, Dwindle; 26, Younger.

No. 31

ACROSS. – 1, Grenade; 8, Avenues; 9, Muggins; 10, Prattle; 11, Edition; 14, Acorns; 18, Sylph; 20, Pagoda; 22, Saddle; 23, Iliad; 25, Ritual; 28, Onerous; 29, Gossips; 32, Lenient; 33, Silence; 34, Steamer.

DOWN. – 1, Gamekeeper; 2, Eggs; 3, Amid; 4, Ensigns; 5, Overlaps; 6, Initio; 7, Merlin; 12, Ingot; 13, India; 15, Chafe; 16, Radio; 17, Stepsister; 19, Yea; 21, Allspice; 24, Doubles; 26, Iconic; 27, Ulster; 30, Ante; 31, Term.

No. 32

ACROSS. – 5, Robust; 8, Vagrancy; 9, Crusty; 10, Hard cash; 11, Optician; 12, Site; 14, Ban; 15, Warder; 16, Set apart; 19, The mayor; 23, Orphan; 26, Inn; 27, Lent; 28, Cold snap; 29, Pleading; 31, Alpaca; 32, Nobleman; 33, Embers.

DOWN. – 1, Malaria; 2, Grudged; 3, Anna; 4, Pythons; 5, Recitation; 6, Blue-cap; 7, Set fair; 12, Swat; 13, True; 14, Braying ass; 17, Ache; 18, Tent; 20, Hoodlum; 21, Mediate; 22, Ripping; 24, Plodder; 25, Ananias; 30, Elbe.

No. 33

ACROSS. – 1, Business; 5, Stop up; 9, Semolina; 11, Sesame; 12, Trap; 13, Cue; 14, Abates; 15, Rose-bowl; 18, Sign; 20, Punch; 21, Seven; 22, Hers; 24, Seconded; 28, Popple; 29, Eel; 30, Mood; 32, Handle; 34, Tenantry; 35, Tierce; 36, Restored.

DOWN. – 1, Bisect; 2, Summer; 3, No less; 4, Sent; 6, Tie; 7, Plantain; 8, Pressing; 10, Argon; 11, Spalpeen; 16, Opus; 17, Excuse me; 18, Sere; 19, Chip-shot; 20, Prepense; 23, Scoot; 25, Depart; 26, Debtor; 27, Flayed; 31, Dene; 33, Lac.

No. 34

ACROSS. – 1, Kick-off; 5, Scribes; 9, Nobel peace prize; 10, Dent; 11, Screw; 12, Flop; 15, Mottled; 16, Sea-kale; 17, Chindit; 19, Bran-tub; 21, Rail; 22, Paris; 23, Juno; 26, Intellectual set; 27, Harness; 28, Rooster.

DOWN. – 1, Kingdom; 2, Cabinet minister; 3, Oily; 4, Fleeced; 5, Suckers; 6, Rope; 7, Brilliant sunset; 8, Steeple; 13, Blade; 14, Banal; 17, Cornish; 18, Teasers; 19, Blister; 20, Bloater; 24, Glee; 25, Faro.

No. 35

ACROSS. – 1, Magisterially; 10, Ovation; 11, One vote; 12, Bite; 13, Huron; 14, Ties; 17, Expiate; 18, Shingle; 19, Exhibit; 22, Parasol; 24, Luge; 25, Silas; 26, Bill; 29, Network; 30, Sunburn; 31, Maitres d'hotel.

DOWN. – 2, At a stop; 3, Isis; 4, Tonsure; 5, Riotous; 6, Ahem; 7, Looking; 8, Double dealing; 9, Lets well alone; 15, Mamba; 16, Fiord; 20, High tea; 21, Trickle; 22, Praised; 23, Seizure; 27, Post; 28, Into.

No. 36

ACROSS. – 1, Fish and chips; 8, Abigail; 9, Non-stop; 11, Ruinous; 12, Scallop; 13, Ingot; 14, Early call; 16, Barnacled; 19, Meter; 21, Numeric; 23, Algebra; 24, Sea-wall; 25, Theoric; 26, Stretched out.

DOWN. – 1, Fairing; 2, Seaport; 3, All is well; 4, Don'ts; 5, Hungary; 6, Patella; 7, Hairpin bends; 10, Popular fancy; 15, Red cattle; 17, Remnant; 18, Acreage; 19, Magneto; 20, Tabaret; 22, Colic.

No. 37

ACROSS. – 7, Prince of Denmark; 8, Aground; 10, Sun-rays; 11, Sable; 12, Idles; 14, Allow; 15, Rats; 16, Wold; 17, Even; 19, Muff; 21, Agile; 22, Tarry; 23, Count; 25, Bassoon; 26, Tobacco; 27, Administrations.

DOWN. – 1, Brigade of Guards; 2, Snooker; 3, Jeans; 4, Revue; 5, Emerald; 6, Greyhound racing; 9, Dais; 10, Slow; 13, Salve; 14, Aloft; 17, Elastic; 18, Noon; 19, Mint; 20, Fanatic; 23, Comic; 24, Today.

No. 38

ACROSS. – 1, Sand-castle; 9, Warn; 10, Dover soles; 11, Twitch; 12, Passage; 15, Angelus; 16, Eland; 17, Sofa; 18, Over; 19, Idler; 21, Old wine; 22, Rostrum; 24, Flight; 27, Instalment; 28, Coke; 29, Leadership.

DOWN. – 2, Agog; 3, Dreams; 4, Assuage; 5, Till; 6, East end; 7, Cantilever; 8, In the scrum; 12, Post Office; 13, Soft drinks; 14, Elide; 15, Anker; 19, Initial; 20, Roulade; 23, Thames; 25, Asia; 26, Anti.

No. 39

ACROSS. – 8, Parasite; 9, Ocular; 10, Metrical; 12, Rebuff; 14, Stay at home; 18, Tara; 21, In point; 22, Redoubt; 23, Tied; 25, Astigmatic; 28, Drones; 30, Antimony; 32, Tailor; 33, Seminary.

DOWN. – 1, Caveat; 2, Fairly; 3, Disc; 4, Meal; 5, Cowrie; 6, Turbot; 7, Calf; 11, Achates; 13, Frantic; 14, Sainted; 15, Apple; 16, Axis; 17, Martian; 19, Adult; 20, Adam; 24, Dingle; 25, Assure; 26, Arming; 27, Ignore; 29, Real; 30, Also; 31, Time.

No. 40

ACROSS. – 1, Popular; 5, Dyke; 9, People in general; 10, Maid; 11, Covet; 12, Inca; 15, Animals; 16, Shuffle; 17, Lagging; 19, Mongrel; 21, Coup; 22, Flame; 23, Wand; 26, Frightened child; 27, Dray; 28, Stringy.

DOWN. – 1, Pip Emma; 2, Promising pupil; 3, Loll; 4, Ruinous; 5, Digress; 6, Kine; 7, Pillage; 8, Transformation; 13, Magic; 14, Burnt; 17, Lucifer; 18, Gallery; 19, Members; 20, Lady Day; 24, Char; 25, Scar.

No. 41

ACROSS. – 4, Dandruff; 8, Vendetta; 9, Dutiable; 10, Punjab; 11, Beseeching; 16, Abel; 18, Are; 19, Moisten; 21, Lance; 22, All in; 23, Start in; 26, Ism; 28, Erie; 29, Easy chairs; 33, Typify; 35, Deputize; 36, Refinery; 37, Fragment.

DOWN. – 1, Menu; 2, Odd jobs; 3, Stubble; 4, Dados; 5, Nether; 6, Reach; 7, Felon; 10, Permeate; 12, Earls; 13, Cellar; 14, Innate; 15, Guernsey; 16, Aisles; 17, Ethnic; 20, Norma; 24, Testify; 25, Ripping; 27, Shrine; 30, Ameer; 31, Young; 32, Inert; 34, Farm.

No. 42

ACROSS. – 1, Caliph; 4, Club; 7, Mown down; 8, Effect; 10, Syringed; 13, Shocks; 14, Gorilla; 15, Unveil; 18, Unbraid; 19, Erring; 20, Minaret; 25, Sampan; 26, Lose face; 27, Rating; 28, Corridor; 29, Rods; 30, Hoarse.

DOWN. – 1, Coward; 2, Lading; 3, Powder; 5, Left hand; 6, Breeches; 7, Mash; 9, Tussle; 11, Going in; 12, Diurnal; 13, Sluices; 16, Censor; 17, Promoter; 18, Unmanned; 21, Rococo; 22, Terror; 23, Candle; 24, Beer.

No. 43

ACROSS. – 1, Seesaw; 5, Better; 10, Torquay; 11, Amnesia; 12, Confer; 15, Arcade; 16, Records; 17, Sash; 18, Cent; 19, Leagues; 20, Apse; 22, Scan; 25, Hurried; 27, Kelpie; 28, Dreams; 31, Emanate; 32, Pigtail; 33, Canyon; 34, Yankee.

DOWN. – 2, Errands; 3, Saucer; 4, Ways; 5, Brag; 6, Tenors; 7, Ensnare; 8, Stocks: 9, Talent; 13, Revenue; 14, Forgery; 15, Adhered; 20, Anklet; 21, Sultana; 23, Charade; 24, Nestle; 25, Hilary; 26, Dragon; 29, Tern; 30, Spry.

No. 44

ACROSS. – 5, Farmer; 8, Maritime; 9, Nimbus; 10, Wistaria; 11, Roasts; 12, Comedian; 15, Lares; 16, Solitary; 19, Canadian; 24, Slain; 27, Untended; 28, Images; 29, Mangling; 30, Bumble; 31, Gruesome; 32, Dynast.

DOWN. – 1, Capitol; 2, Vintner; 3, Milreis; 4, Remains; 5, Funeral; 6, Rampart; 7, Equator; 13, Main; 14, Dead; 17, Isle; 18, Arid; 20, Armoury; 21, Algebra; 22, Inspect; 23, Nutmegs; 24, Stand up; 25, Analyse; 26, New name.

No. 45

ACROSS. – 1, Marocain; 5, Stable; 9, Dark Ages; 10, Oxtail; 12, Catherine; 13, Medoc; 14, Heel; 16, Artisan; 19, Malison; 21, Care; 24, Straw; 25, Dungarees; 27, At heel; 28, Automata; 29, Yawned; 30, Prudence.

DOWN. – 1, Medico; 2, Rarity; 3, Clare; 4, Ice-hill; 6, Taximeter; 7, Blandish; 8, Enlacing; 11, Lena; 15, Elsewhere; 17, Emissary; 18, Clerihew; 20, Nude; 21, Conquer; 22, Petain; 23, Escape; 26, Aloud.

No. 46

ACROSS. – 1, Doormat; 5, Bramble; 9, Middle of the road; 10, Loan; 11, Spell; 12, Adze; 15, Scholar; 16, Strands; 17, Mordant; 19, Washtub; 21, Soho; 22, Windy; 23, Buns; 26, Common knowledge; 27, Last man; 28, Kestrel

DOWN. – 1, Dimples; 2, Old Father Thames; 3, Mole; 4, Trooper; 5, Bottles; 6, Ales; 7, Blood and thunder; 8, Endless; 13, Cloak; 14, Brass; 17, Musical; 18, Thicken; 19, Wedlock; 20, Boswell; 24, Boom; 25, Alas.

No. 47

ACROSS. – 8, A real man; 9, Ultimo; 10, Old boy; 11, Cannibal; 12, Hearse; 13, Energies; 15, Acre; 17, Piscina; 19, Statute; 22, Late; 24, After all; 27, Slalom; 29, Ballyhoo; 30, Collar; 31, Lesion; 32, Observer.

DOWN. – 1, Grilse; 2, Barbaric; 3, Empyrean; 4, Knocker; 5, Quince; 6, String; 7, Immanent; 14, Nest; 16, Call; 18, Infra red; 20, Test case; 21, Trailers; 23, Alcohol; 25, Eclair; 26, Aching; 28, Onager.

No. 48

ACROSS. – 1, Pit-a-pat; 5, Hack-saw; 9, Romance; 10, Warrant; 11, Birthdays; 12, Sylph; 13, Enter; 15, Lawn-mower; 17, Income-tax; 19, Scarf; 22, Peron; 23, Smothered; 25, Trefoil; 26, Embrace; 27, Stand-in; 28, Satiety.

DOWN. – 1, Parable; 2, Tamerat; 3, Punch; 4, The ballet; 5, Hawks; 6, Christmas; 7, Swallow; 8, Watcher; 14, Roman Road; 16, Wax models; 17, Impetus; 18, Carnera; 20, Air base; 21, Fidgety; 23, Salon; 24, Habit.

No. 49

ACROSS. – 1, Pumas; 4, Back-slang; 9, Parsnip; 11, Ravages; 12, Eton; 13, Stain; 14, Ally; 17, Primary colour; 19, Ancient lights; 21, Cage; 22, Oscar; 23, Otto; 26, Calypso; 27, Neither; 28, Increases; 29, Medoc.

DOWN. – 1, Pepper-pot; 2, Marconi; 3, Sink; 5, Corridor train; 6, Save; 7, Angular; 8, Gusty; 10, Petty sessions; 15, Farce; 16, Motif; 18, Bishopric; 19, Angelic; 20 Hatched; 21, Cacti; 24, Opie; 25, Firm.

No. 50

ACROSS. – 1, Account; 5, Musk-rat; 9, Parliamentarian; 10, Acid; 11, Pedal; 12, Snub; 15, Segment; 16, Expanse; 17, Pea soup; 19, Bahamas; 21, Lady; 22, Spoon; 23, Onus; 26, Chapter and verse; 27, Narrows; 28, Earthed.

DOWN. – 1, Appeals; 2, Carriage and pair; 3, Unit; 4, Tempest; 5, Mundane; 6, Spar; 7, Reigning monarch; 8, Tenable; 13, Decoy; 14, Spahi; 17, Pelican; 18, Papyrus; 19, Brownie; 20, Suspend; 24, Otto; 25, Over.

No. 51

ACROSS. – 1, Tartar; 4, Abnormal; 9, Indeed; 10, Anisette; 12, Lucca; 13, Wood-smoke; 15, Nee; 16, Tweed; 17, Arrack; 20, Rut; 22, Ego; 25, Ransom; 26, Leach; 29, Arc; 30, Coalition; 33, Order; 34, Outburst; 35, Chorea; 36, Tampered; 37, Granny.

DOWN. – 1, Triolets; 2, Redacted; 3, Alexandra; 5, Banjo; 6, Oasis; 7, Method; 8, Leered; 11, Sweats; 14, Drag; 18, Remand; 19, Colcothar; 21, Unit; 23, Mandarin; 24, Pharmacy; 27, Accost; 28, Bantam; 31, Inure; 32, Issue.

No. 52

ACROSS. – 1, Fortunate; 9, Cornet; 10, Wednesday; 11, Street; 12, Boundless; 13, Chisel; 17, Tip; 19, Back-stage nerves; 20, Bun; 21, Nearly; 25, Paragraph; 26, Amiens; 27, Milk shake; 28, Cloudy; 29, Underdone.

DOWN. – 2, Oberon; 3, Tenant; 4, Nestle; 5, Transfiguration; 6, Lost sheep; 7, Intensive; 8, Stateless; 14, Abundance; 15, Scrap iron; 16, Esplanade; 17, Tab; 18, Pen; 22, Tackle; 23, Arched; 24, Spoken.

No. 53

ACROSS. – 1, Red lane; 5, Gullets; 9, Fight; 10, Blister; 11, Rur; 12, Aroma; 13, Emergency; 16, Ken; 17, Notch; 18, Booster; 20, Parangs; 23, Bower; 26, Col; 27, Right bank; 31, Icing; 32, Hue; 33, Invited; 34, Taste; 35, Lanolin; 36, Duennas.

DOWN. – 1, Refrain; 2, Digs out; 3, Astrakhan; 4, Entre nous, 5, Gable; 6, Lying; 7, Eaton; 8, Sprayer; 14, Rio; 15, Ems; 18, Blockhead; 19, Oubliette; 20, Partial; 21, Ash; 22, Gab; 24, Whitsun; 25, Regress; 28, Given; 29, Total; 30, Arden.

No. 54

ACROSS. – 8, Popular air; 9, Gala; 10, Bird of prey; 11, Lamb; 12, Rocket-line; 17, Cleek; 20, Seen; 21, Pump; 23, Blank; 24, Strange men; 30, Cube; 31, Marked time; 32, Lien; 33, Legal light.

DOWN. – 1, Solid; 2, Sundries; 3, Gaffer; 4, Fabric; 5, Groyne; 6, Hawaii; 7, Bauble; 13, Ounce; 14, Kopje; 15, Tomb; 16, Noon; 18, Loft; 19, Kern, 22, Plantain; 24, Sickle; 25, Rubber; 26, Gamble; 27, Mirage; 28, Needle; 29, Omaha.

No. 55

ACROSS. – 1, Haberdasher; 9, Eclat; 10, Peregrinate; 11, Dinar; 12, State; 15, Types; 17, Ale; 18, Jehu; 19, Goods; 21, Talon; 22, Cubic; 23, Strap; 26, Hope; 27, Elf; 28, Joker; 30, Fists; 33, Reeve; 35, Thoughtless; 36, Treat; 37, Yellow press.

DOWN. – 2, Avert; 3, Eject; 4, Dory; 5, Sandy; 6, Reeds; 7, Blunder-buss; 8, Stirrup-cups; 12, Scotch broth; 13, Apple-pie bed; 14, Earns; 15, Teg; 16, End; 20, Scoff; 24, Too; 25, Per; 28, Jetty; 29, Equal; 31, Idler; 32, Tests; 34, Dhow.

No. 56

ACROSS. – 1, Dry martini; 9, Rush; 10, Court dress; 11, Exeter; 12, Eclat; 15, Gears; 18, Eerie; 19, Canvass; 20, Ratio; 21, Shine; 22, Realise; 23, Eagre; 24, Naked; 26, Crust; 29, Slater; 31, Artichokes; 32, Ache; 33, Perishable.

DOWN. – 2, Roof; 3, Murder; 4, Ridge; 5, Ideal; 6, Inset; 7, Butter-milk; 8, Sharper end; 13, Centaur; 14, Ananias; 15, Garden seat; 16, Autographs; 17, Score; 18, Essen; 25, Aurora; 26, Cramp; 27, Utter; 28, Ticks; 30, Well.

No. 57

ACROSS. —5, HAC; 8, Stonehenge; 9, Hair; 10, Encouraged; 11, Fort; 12, Blubber; 16, Concept; 17, Decoy; 18, Probe; 19, Baton; 20, Virus; 22, Persian; 23, Stifled; 26, Grit; 27, Inside left; 30, Here; 31, Nigrescent; 32, Rat.

DOWN – 1, Eton; 2, Into; 3, Charted; 4, Snags; 5, Head boy; 6, Chiffchaff; 7, Microphone; 10, Ebb; 13, Large order; 14, Baby-sitter; 15, Resin; 16, Comus; 20, Variant; 21, Studied; 24, Dot; 25, Usage; 28, Lock; 29, Fine.

No. 58

ACROSS. – 1, Bran tub; 5, Depicts; 9, Release; 10, Cantata; 11, Newmarket; 12, Piece; 13, Tudor; 15, Attribute; 17, Attracted; 19, Lupin; 22, Fling; 23, Following; 25, Outrage; 26, Alabama; 27, Tuesday; 28, East end.

DOWN. – 1, Baronet; 2, Allowed; 3, Tiara; 4, Breakfast; 5, Ducat; 6, Pin-up girl; 7, Chateau; 8, Siamese; 14, Rearguard; 16, Tidal wave; 17, Affront; 18, Thistle; 20, Private; 21, Niggard; 23, Fiery; 24, Opals.

No. 59

ACROSS. –1, Endows; 4, Spiteful; 9, Clinic; 10, Undercut; 12, Maple; 13, Melodious; 15, Lap; 16, Ennui; 17, Gaby; 19, Nil; 21, Are; 24, Dene; 25, Adieu; 28, Act; 29, Something; 32, At sea; 33, Bouncing; 34, Tooley; 35, Erectors; 36, Street.

DOWN. – 1, Encumber; 2, Dripping; 3, White line; 5, Panel; 6, Trend; 7, Factor; 8, Latest; 11, Impale; 14, Omar; 17, Garage; 18, Beat about; 20, Inch; 22, Dissolve; 23, Rubaiyat; 26, Usable; 27, Immure; 30, Tacit; 31, Inner.

No. 60

ACROSS. – 1, Under water; 9, Polo; 10, Flood-gates; 11, Castle; 12, Man-hunt; 15, Seringa; 16, Grand; 17, Neck; 18, Mint; 19, Genus; 21, Flowers; 22, Thinner; 24, Extend; 27, Decapitate; 28, Numb; 29, Elder-berry.

DOWN. – 2, Nile; 3, Enough; 4, Wagging; 5, Tots; 6, Rescued; 7, Contention; 8, Covenanter; 12, Man of means; 13, Nick of time; 14, Trees; 15, Snout; 19, Griddle; 20, Sharper; 23, Nettle; 25, Acid; 26, Star.

No. 61

ACROSS. – 1, Cor anglais; 9, Nero; 10, Safety lamp; 11, Potion; 12, Hawsers; 15, Predict; 16, Start; 17, Cast; 18, Skye; 19, Cream; 21, Saintly; 22, Marvell; 24, Orgies; 27, Tantamount; 28, Upon; 29, Restaurant.

DOWN. – 2, Oval; 3, Agents; 4, Geysers; 5, Adam; 6, Support; 7, Periwinkle; 8, Down-at-heel; 12, Hocus-pocus; 13, Washington; 14, Story; 15, Priam; 19, Cluster; 20, Marsala; 23, Vigour; 25, Inns; 26, Anon.

No. 62

ACROSS. – 1, Bloater; 5, Reclaim; 9, Bats in the belfry; 10, Joey; 11, Bonus; 12, Zero; 15, Bristle; 16, Kitchen; 17, Athlete; 19, Praised; 21, Ally; 22, Spray; 23, Adam; 26, Money for nothing; 27, Dessert; 28, Red-eyed.

Down. – 1, Bob-a-job; 2, On the right lines; 3, Trip; 4, Rat-hole; 5, Roebuck; 6, Chef; 7, As fresh as a daisy; 8, May morn; 13, Steel; 14, Stoat; 17, Alarmed; 18, Exploit; 19, Planner; 20, Damaged; 24, Tyre; 25, Stud.

No. 63

Across. – 1, Bath chair; 6, Comma; 9, Saxophone; 10, Bogus; 11, Dor; 12, Congeries; 15, Icing; 16, Magus; 19, Fugal; 21, Use, 22, Lie; 23, Barge; 24, Tress; 26, Groat; 27, Pendragon; 31, Air; 32, Aping; 33, Integrate; 35, Tunis; 36, Eightsome.

Down. – 1, Basic; 2, Toxin; 3, Copse; 4, Ago; 5, Reeds; 6, Cabriolet; 7, Magnitude; 8, Assignees; 13, Gnu; 14, Infer; 16, Malignant; 17, Gregorian; 18, Sabotages; 20, Green; 25, R.M.A.; 27, Prime; 28, Right; 29, Guano; 30, Niece; 34, Teg.

No. 64

Across. – 1, Beauty spot; 8, Repeal; 9, Art gallery; 10, Animal; 11, Flickering; 12, Antler; 13, Peri; 15, Dead Sea; 19, On trial; 21, Stud; 22, Big gap; 25, Everything; 27, Arctic; 28, Identified; 29, Attila; 30, Lightships.

Down. – 1, Bradford; 2, Attain; 3, Thanks; 4, Solar; 5, Try again; 6, Splinter; 7, Pasadena; 13, Pat; 14, Rod; 16, Emigrate; 17, Dogs tail; 18, Especial; 20, Long odds; 23, Stairs; 24, Bikini; 26, Ranch.

No. 65

Across. – 1, Divers; 4, Dakota; 10, Rangoon; 11, Harness; 12, Her; 13, Drama; 14, Drear; 15, Deferentially; 18, Carpet-baggers; 23, Elope; 25, Fiver; 26, Nor; 27, Postern; 28, Engages; 29, Sedate; 30, Studio.

Down. – 1, Deride; 2, Vantage; 3, Rhoda; 5, Aired; 6, One bell; 7, Absorb; 8, An honest penny; 9, Christmas tree; 16, Fir; 17, Lie; 19, Aroused; 20, Ravaged; 21, Tempus; 22, Presto; 24, Event; 25, Fugit.

No. 66

Across. – 1, Tropics; 5, Shelter; 9, Break break break; 10, Lute; 11, Falls; 12, Solo; 15, Ratline; 16, Thicket; 17, Toe-caps; 19, Sign off; 21, Plug; 22, Punch; 23, Glen; 26, Colourful border; 27, Lecture; 28, Run well.

Down. – 1, Tubular; 2, Open to the public; 3, Inky; 4, Surface; 5, Scarlet; 6. Elbe; 7, Tree of knowledge; 8, Rake out; 13, Rival; 14, Dingy; 17, Typical; 18, Shuffle; 19, Secular; 20, Funeral; 24, Zulu; 25, Born.

No. 67.

Across. – 1, Field Marshal; 8, Alabama; 9, Strokes; 12, Etch; 13, Poker; 14, Dali; 17, Discern; 18, Sun-dial; 19, Opening; 22, Cutlass; 24, Plan; 25, Inane; 26, Idea; 29, Red deer; 31, Embroil; 32, Small letters.

Down. – 1, Francis; 2, Edam; 3, Dragoon; 4, Answers; 5, Sort; 6, Lee; 7, Eavesdropper; 10, Khaki; 11, Shilly-shally; 15, Lenin; 16, Unite; 20, Eland; 21, General; 22, Content; 23, Arduous, 27, Well; 28, Able; 30, Ems.

No. 68

Across. – 1, Catherine; 8, Letters Patent; 11, Needs; 12, Drown; 13, Seats; 16, Enrich; 17, Heckle; 18, Outre; 19, Toss-up; 20, Exeats; 21, Strut; 24, Thing; 26, Waltz; 27, Lady of the lake; 28, Frankness.

Down. – 2, Altos; 3, Hurdle; 4, Rupert; 5, Noted; 6, Cerebro-spinal; 7, Unworkmanlike; 9, Intestate, 10, Under size; 13, Shops; 14, Altar; 15, Sheet; 22, Tiffin; 23, Urchin; 25, Gayer; 26, Wales.

No. 69

Across. – 1, Lochinvar; 6, Pupil; 9, Celluloid; 10, Latin; 11, Dromedary; 14, China; 15, Hebe; 16, Temple; 19, Maize; 20, Iron ore; 22, Admit; 23, Inject; 24, Eros; 26, Trier; 27, Pheasants; 32, Ariel; 33, Quibbling; 34, Kiddy; 35, Exactness.

Down. – 1, Lucid; 2, Cello; 3, Inure; 4, Viola; 5, Red dye; 6, Policemen; 7, Patricide; 8, Land agent; 12, Doer; 13, Rhenish; 16, Toast-rack; 17, Mummified; 18, Literally; 21, Rima; 25, Opaque; 28, Erica; 29, Sabot; 30, Noise; 31, Signs.

No. 70

Across. – 1, County town; 8, Evelyn; 9, Absconding; 10 Averse; 11, Plagiarist; 12, Indite; 13, Oslo; 15, Erosion; 19, Encrust; 21, Rent; 22, Ending; 25, Allowances; 27, Jerkin; 28, Intimidate; 29, Jumbos; 30, Thunderous.

Down. – 1, Clay pipe; 2, Unseat; 3, Tropic; 4, Tudor; 5, Negation; 6, Defender; 7, Myosotis; 13, One; 14, Let; 16, Runner-up; 17, Sticks by; 18, Organist; 20, Trustees; 23, Valise; 24, Octavo; 26, Onion.

No. 71

Across. – 1, Pomiculture; 7, Grenade; 8, Release; 10, Neat; 11, Stoat; 13, Epee; 15, Ant; 17, Ardent; 19, Egbert; 20, Ear-ring; 21, Mincer; 23, Domino; 25, Cub; 27, Rent; 28, Basle; 29, Nisi; 32, En-large; 33, Trailer; 24, Sympathizes.

Down. – 1, Piebald; 2, Meal; 3, Cresta; 4, Lariat; 5, Ugly; 6, Example; 7, Gendarmerie; 9, Electrolier; 12, Onerous; 14, Sneer; 16, Egg on; 18, Tar; 19, End; 22, Nonplus; 24, Icicles; 25, Camera; 26, Blotch; 30, Dram; 31, Jazz.

No. 72

Across. – 1, Alcoran; 5, Goat; 9, Heir to the throne; 10, Eddy; 11, Flask; 12, True; 15, Emerged; 16, Dull wit; 17, Fastnet; 19, Mean-der; 21, Rout; 22, Snags; 23, Clef; 26, Discovered by man; 27, Stay; 28, Spenser.

Down. – 1, Athlete; 2, Children's nurse; 3, Rate; 4, Nettled; 5, Guessed; 6, Ache; 7, Present; 8, Borrowed plumes; 13, Agony; 14, Float; 17, Faraday; 18, Tannery; 19, Magnets; 20, Refiner; 24, Coot; 25, Abbe.

No. 73

Across. – 2, Pillar to post; 8, Tool; 9, Upright piano; 10, From; 12, Caulk; 14, Blast; 17, Offal; 18, Cut in; 19, Santa; 20, Corps; 21, Neath; 22, Elemi; 23, Genre; 26, Smear; 30, Once; 32, Breaking step; 33, Acre; 34, Mythological.

Down. – 1, Four; 2, Plum; 3, Larva; 4, Argil; 5, Tate; 6, Phial; 7, Sands; 10, Foot-slog; 11, Off and on; 12, Cleanse; 13, Ketch; 14, Bencher; 15, Aberdeen; 16, Thuswise; 18, Claus; 24, Early; 25, Reach; 27, Magog; 28, Antic; 29, Pill; 30, Opal; 31, Cork.

No. 74

Across. – 8, Parisian; 9, Ripper; 10, Chopping; 12, Daring; 14, Vulnerable; 18, Tell; 21, Suicide; 22, Gun-site; 23, Buds; 25, Stationary; 28, Emerge; 30, Hypnosis; 32, Friend; 33, Fusilier.
Down. – 1, Cachou; 2, Gilpin; 3, Fifi; 4, Snug; 5, Cradle; 6, Spirit; 7, Rein; 11, Nearest; 13, Gallery; 14, Visible; 15, Laird; 16, Exit; 17, Lightly; 19, Erica; 20, Into; 24, Survey; 25, Steady; 26, Noodle; 27, Raised; 29, Mark; 30, Huff; 31, Push.

No. 75

Across. – 8, Hero; 9, One; 10, In time; 11, Flotow; 12, Vitality; 13, The artful dodger; 15, At least; 17, Fylfots; 20, From i. and to mouth; 23, Sporadic; 25, Office; 26, Poteen; 27, Tar; 28, Lied.
Down. – 1, Health; 2, Boat-race; 3, Notwithstanding; 4, Nervous; 5, Birthday honours; 6, Styled; 7, Emit; 14, Eat; 16, Tor; 18, Footfall; 19, Educate; 21, Merger; 22, Ticket; 24, Pros.

No. 76

Across. – 1, Dunderhead; 8, Eaglet; 9, Jackanapes; 10, Orrery; 11, Uneventful; 12, Arenas; 13, Chat; 15, Rotunda; 19, Celeste; 21, Emit; 22, Stable; 25, Masquerade; 27, Scones; 28, Threatened; 29, Battle; 30, Restrained.
Down. – 1, Dejeuner; 2, Nickel; 3, Enamel; 4, Heart; 5, Desolate; 6, Aggrieve; 7, Recreant; 13, Cam; 14, Act; 16, Optician; 17, Urbanity; 18, Deemster; 20, Extended; 23, Bertha; 24, Cannon; 26, Quest.

No. 77

Across. – 1, Handle-bars; 6, Clod; 10, Paris; 11, Cannibals; 12, Claymore; 13, Press; 15, Manhunt; 17, Scrooge; 19, Lasting; 21, Prefect; 22, Ouida; 24, Steerage; 27, Totem-pole; 28, Booth; 29, Rare; 30, Ascendency.
Down. – 1, Hops; 2, Nurslings; 3, Lusty; 4, Back out; 5, Runners; 7, Lease; 8, Dust-sheets; 9, Disperse; 14, Smell of tar; 16, Up in arms; 18, Overgrown; 20, Gaseous; 21, Precede; 23, Inter; 25, Rabid; 26, Shay.

No. 78

Across. – 5, Public; 8, Belittle; 9, Rounds; 10, Unafraid; 11, Outlay; 12, Decision; 15, Salon; 16, Grafting; 19, Blow-lamp; 24, Sweep; 27, Tennyson; 28, Tomtom; 29, Lifebelt; 30, Cigale; 31, Militant; 32, Census.
Down. – 1, Peonies; 2, Tinfoil; 3, Stearin; 4, Bedding; 5, Pergola; 6, Blue-tit; 7, Indrawn; 13, Cato; 14, Soil; 17, Fawn; 18, Ides; 20, Leonine; 21, Wet days; 22, Aimless; 23, Ptolemy; 24, Snaffle; 25, Eye-bath; 26, Polling.

No. 79

ACROSS. – 1, Four-poster; 8, Exam; 10, Paratroops; 11, Abel; 12, Tomb; 15, Measles; 18, Nacre; 19, Caleb; 20, Tiger; 21, Rolls; 22, Angel; 23, Incur; 24, Satan; 25, Eaton; 26, Actress; 30, Sirs; 33, Coda; 34, Carrying on; 35, Menu; 36, Motherwell.

DOWN. – 2, Oval; 3, Reade; 4, Ogres; 5, Those; 6, Rest; 7, Maim; 9, Mannerisms; 10, Percolator; 13, Obligation; 14, Babylonian; 15, Messina; 16, Leger; 17, Scrapes; 20, Tacit; 27, Caret; 28, Rhyme; 29, Sinew; 31, Item; 32, Scum; 33, Coil.

No. 80

ACROSS. – 1, Model; 4, Trumpeter; 9, Lobelia; 10, Shallow; 11, Dace; 12, Stoat; 13, Pony; 16, Atelier; 17, Twisted; 19, Andante; 22, Francis; 24, Peel; 25, Egham; 26, Snug; 29, Rossini; 30, Indiana; 31, Horseshoe; 32, Nurse.

DOWN. – 1, Melodrama; 2, Debacle; 3, Lily; 4, Tractor; 5, Upstart; 6, Peak; 7, Talk out; 8, Rowdy; 14, Giant; 15, Midas; 18, Designate; 20, Dresser; 21, English; 22, Fragile; 23, Centaur; 24, Porch; 27, Wine; 28, Odin.

No. 81

ACROSS. – 1, Deposition; 6, Aces; 9, Contraband; 10, Smee; 13, Repaint; 15, Broker; 16, Gimlet; 17, Inferior article; 18, Absent; 20, Crater; 21, Guerdon; 22, Iris; 25, Grub Street; 26, Nine; 27, Staying put.

DOWN. – 1, Dock; 2, Punt; 3, Server; 4, To be a farmer's boy; 5, Owning; 7, Complicate; 8, Sweetheart; 11, Obligation; 12, Confession; 13, Rearing; 14, Tintern; 19, Turret; 20, Cotton; 23, Weep; 24, Stet.

No. 82

ACROSS. – 1, Decrepitude; 9, Hale; 10, Finger-print; 11, Camp; 14, Meddles; 18, Above; 19, Amain; 20, Ate; 21, Pal; 22, Digit; 23, Teeth; 24, Tee; 26, Ski; 27, Irene; 28, Reign; 29, Adulate; 33, Heal; 36, Sententious; 37, Aden; 38, Preparatory.

DOWN. – 2, Exit; 3, Rage; 4, Perse; 5, Tired; 6, Dante; 7, Camaraderie; 8, Helping hand; 12, Sandwich-man; 13, Congregated; 14, Meat tea; 15, Die; 16, Lip; 17, Saltire; 25, Emu; 26, Sea; 30, Drear; 31, Lit up; 32, Tuner; 34, Wilt; 35, Burr.

No. 83

ACROSS. – 1, Marbles; 5, Burgher; 9, Hoe; 10, Trickle; 11, Left arm; 12, Laws; 13, Trained man; 15, Dry land; 17, Matinee; 19, Retiled; 22, Chowder; 25, Chief scout; 26, Frog; 28, Rossini; 29, Amiable; 30, Nod; 31, Speckle; 32, Express.

DOWN. – 1, Mottled; 2, Railway; 3, Lake; 4, Sheared; 5, Belgium; 6, Reflection; 7, Headman; 8, Romance; 14, Pail of milk; 16, Rue; 18, Eve; 19, Records; 20, Trieste; 21, Decline; 22, Crusade; 23, Durable; 24, Regrets; 27, Gimp.

No. 84

ACROSS. – 1, Fly-catcher; 9, Mesh; 10, Broad views; 11, Trivet; 12, Passing; 15, Feather; 16, Sower; 17, Sore; 18, Laic; 19, Creep; 21, Existed; 22, Recital; 24, Grease; 27, Avaricious; 28, Road; 29, Stony stare.

DOWN. – 2, Lure; 3, Chains; 4, Taverns; 5, Heed; 6, Rustler; 7, Heavy heart; 8, Rhetorical; 12, Passengers; 13, Serviceman; 14, Gourd; 15, Fever; 19, Cereals; 20, Petrify; 23, Indict; 25, Halo; 26, Purr.

No. 85

ACROSS. – 1, Second childhood; 9, Existed; 10, Hairpin; 11, Kirk; 12, Eclat; 13, Here; 16, Nuptial; 17, Lock-nut; 18, Tickets; 21, Capable; 23, Urns; 24, Sieve; 25, Hard; 28, Prosper; 29, Murrain; 30, Turns up one's nose.

DOWN. – 1, Speaking-trumpet; 2, Chirrup; 3, Note; 4, Codicil; 5, Ishmael; 6, Dail; 7, Orphean; 8, Dance attendance; 14, Tides; 15, Scope; 19, Contour; 20, Stirrup; 21, Caveman; 22, Bravado; 26, Opus; 27, Arks.

No. 86

ACROSS. – 1, Crambo; 4, Spot; 7, Particle; 8, Helmet; 10, Presumed; 13, Detour; 14, Sat upon; 15, Straws; 18, Witless; 19, Persia; 20, Scorned; 25, Grates; 26, Derelict; 27, Thatch; 28, Stalwart; 29, Keep; 30, Ferret.

DOWN. – 1, Carver; 2, Animus; 3, Bullet; 5, Prevents; 6, Temporal; 7, Pips; 9, Thrush; 11, Maniacs; 12, Dullard; 13, Dossier; 16, Spigot; 17, Great auk; 18, Wiseacre; 21, Nestle; 22, Dealer; 23, Dinant; 24, Stot.

No. 87

ACROSS. – 1, Ballot; 4, Arm-in-arm; 9, Newest; 10, Hathaway; 12, Fluff; 13, Australia; 15, Rat; 16, Delta; 17, Cake; 21, Ween; 24, Utter; 27, Yet; 28, Celluloid; 31, Stain; 32, Recreate; 33, Borneo; 34, Hyde Park; 35, Adored.

DOWN. – 1, Bona fide; 2, Lawfully; 3, Ossifrage; 5, Roads; 6, Ichor; 7, As well; 8, May-day; 11, Kate; 14, Tea; 18, Knutsford; 19, Strainer; 20, Cranford; 22, Ell; 23, Hyde; 25, Scorch; 26, Sliced; 29, Use up; 30, Outer.

No. 88

ACROSS. – 1, Piquant; 5, Cogs; 9, The bloom of youth; 10, Hart; 11, Ebony; 12, Gill; 15, Private; 16, Drifter; 17, Chuckle; 19, Patient; 21, Path; 22, Brunt; 23, Limb; 26, Booking the order; 27, Bend; 28, Reflect.

DOWN. – 1, Patch up; 2, Queer situation; 3, Able; 4, Trouble; 5, Crowned; 6, Guys; 7, Scholar; 8, Put in the middle; 13, Tacky; 14, Ditty; 17, Capable; 18, Enraged; 19, Panther; 20, Tabaret; 24, Tile; 25, Roof.

No. 89

ACROSS. – 1, Anthelion; 9, Armoury; 10, Makes up; 11, Astrict; 12, Cattle pen; 14, Pantheon; 15, Carpet; 17, Secundo; 20, Antler; 23, Bootlace; 25, Atrocious; 26, Impends; 27, Plaints; 28, Griddle; 29, Whistlers.

DOWN.-2, Niagara; 3, Heel-tap; 4, Laureate; 5, Nagana; 6, Imitation; 7, Jupiter; 8, Bystander; 13, Epaulet; 15, Cambridge; 16, Esplanade; 18, Damocles; 19, Morphia; 21, Trivial; 22, Equator; 24, Cashew.

No. 90

ACROSS. – 1, Pom-poms; 5, Pitcher; 9, Tarnish; 10, Fancied; 11, In the fray; 12, Epode; 13, Kilts; 15, Condensed; 17, Royal blue; 19, Spars; 22, Downs; 23, Suffocate; 25, Animate; 26, Climate; 27, Pigskin; 28, Summary.

DOWN. – 1, Patrick; 2, Marital; 3, Olive; 4, Spherical; 5, Puffy; 6, Tenseness; 7, Heinous; 8, Red lead; 14, Sales talk; 16, No effects; 17, Red lamp; 18, Yawning; 20, Alabama; 21, Scenery; 23, Sheen; 24, Odium.

No. 91

ACROSS. – 1, Patience; 5, Cassia; 10, So few; 11, Raleigh; 12, Alb; 13, Their; 14, Broadmoor; 16, Taxied; 17, Shapely; 20, Askance; 23, Cat-nap; 26, Uppingham; 29, Ralph; 30, Inc; 31, Terence; 32, Togas; 33, Relish; 34, Black-out.

DOWN. – 1, Pushtu; 2, Taffeta; 3, Edwardian; 4, Crabbed; 6, Ailed; 7, Sligo; 8, Ashtrays; 9, Grooms; 15, Map; 18, Antarctic; 19, Baluster; 21, Ali; 22, Echoed; 23, Comical; 24, Allegro; 25, Whisht; 27, Peril; 28, Nines.

No. 92

ACROSS. – 1, Strife; 4, Efts; 7, Drifting; 8, Plumed; 10, Nihilist; 13, Psalms; 14, Entreat; 15, Cotton; 18, Worship; 19, Askari; 20, Acclaim; 25, Ermine; 26, Escapade; 27, Trials; 28, Pullover; 29, Gore; 30, Hector.

DOWN. – 1, Slight; 2, Rattle; 3, Finest; 5, Full stop; 6, Simulate; 7, Dent; 9, Dosing; 11, Invoice; 12, Trestle; 13, Pacific, 16, Patent; 17, Skimming; 18, Wrangler; 21, Astute; 22, Mallet; 23, Carver; 24, Weir.

No. 93

ACROSS. – 6, Choir-organ; 8, Moab; 9, Tasmanian; 11, Eats; 12, Nil; 13, Immodesty; 16, Said; 17, Adjunct; 18, Courage; 20, Late; 21, Mealtimes; 23, Hap; 24, Echo; 25, Order-book; 29, Bute; 30, Elliptical.

DOWN. – 1, Whit; 2, Kiss; 3, Soya; 4, Ugliest; 5, Cartridges; 7, Nanny-goat; 8, Maelstrom; 10, M.V.O.; 13, Indian club; 14, Mousehole; 15, Decompose; 19, Hardily; 22, I.D.B.; 26, Rope; 27, Ohio; 28, Knap.

No. 94

ACROSS. – 1, Pint of beer; 9, Boot; 10, Weak-willed; 11, Infirm; 12, Hirsute; 15, Partial; 16, Easel; 17, Mist; 18, Lift; 19, Sleep; 21, Nine day; 22, Refined; 24, Enmity; 27, Elucidated; 28, Gong; 29, Satisfying.

DOWN. – 2, Ices; 3, Tokens; 4, Frigate; 5, Ells; 6, Radical; 7, Politician; 8, Stimulated; 12, Ham and eggs; 13, Resentment; 14, Early; 15, Peter; 19, Sawyers; 20, Permits; 23, Infamy; 25, Punt, 26, Seen.

No. 95

ACROSS. – 1, Percheron; 9, Grebe; 10, Pikestaff; 11, Tulip; 12, Neath; 14, Crepe; 16, Tier; 19, Retract; 21, Radio; 22, Overt; 23, Needles; 24, Eros; 25, Speed; 27, Islet; 30, Roach; 32, Tasteless; 33, Drill; 34, Deep field.

DOWN. – 2, Elite; 3, Cheat; 4, Etty; 5, Offer; 6, Agate; 7, Well-timed; 8, Temperate; 13, Heron; 14, Cats-eye; 15, Enabled; 17, Free trade; 18, Idiomatic; 20, Tosti; 25, Shell; 26, Evade; 28, Salmi; 29, Easel; 31, Stop.

No. 96

ACROSS. – 1, Bottles; 5, Dust; 9, William of Orange; 10, Thin; 11, Haunt; 12, Knob; 15, Highway; 16, Earache; 17, Gehenna; 19, Channel; 21, Nuts; 22, Spout; 23, Sign; 26, Reliable service; 27, Beta; 28, Learned.

DOWN. – 1, Bewitch; 2, Telling the tale; 3, Loin; 4, Summary; 5, Defence; 6, Sark; 7, Tremble; 8, On one condition; 13, Swing; 14, Dream; 17, General; 18, Ampulla; 19, Counsel; 20, Linseed; 24, Face; 25 Aria.

No. 97

ACROSS. – 1, Burnt down; 9, Rover; 10, Armaments; 11, Arrow; 12, Spahi; 14, Prank; 16, Mien; 19, Gloated; 21, Lingo; 22, Ellis; 23, Tiercel; 24, News; 25, Serve; 27, Erase; 30, Apeak; 32, Stromboli; 33, Night; 34, Cheapside.

DOWN. – 2, Unrip; 3, Neath; 4, Doer; 5, Water; 6, Break; 7, Avert-ible; 8, Crows-nest; 13, Ingot; 14, Pioneer; 15, Article; 17, Plantains; 18, Knowledge; 20, Delve; 25, Skate; 26, Vetch; 28, Robes; 29, Solid; 31, Soda.

No. 98

ACROSS. – 1, Fifth; 4, Pussy cat; 10, Truckle; 11, In haste; 12, Lime; 13, Umber; 14, Beat; 17, Sixes and sevens; 19, Parallel forces; 22, Arch; 23, Aglow; 24, Mute; 27, Plastic; 28, Nibbled; 29, Capriole; 30, Eased.

DOWN. – 1, Fatalist; 2, Flummox; 3, Hake; 5, Universal joint; 6, Soho; 7, Cistern; 8, Tweet; 9, Terminological; 15, Asian; 16, Avion; 18, Ascended; 20, Arc-lamp; 21, Caudles; 22, Aspic; 25, Etui; 26, Able.

No. 99

ACROSS. – 5, Glance; 8, Drawback; 9, Pandora; 10, Spoor; 11, Eagle-eyed; 13, Amateurs; 14, Nicety; 17, Ham; 19, Egg; 20, Leg-bye; 23, Napoleon; 26, Cormorant; 28, Aspic; 29, Riposte; 30, Practice; 31, Talent.

DOWN. – 1, Odessa; 2, Samovar; 3, Abernethy; 4, Scorer; 5, Gray-ling; 6, Addle; 7, Corvette; 12, Asp; 15, Ignorance; 16, Senorita; 18, Aegrotat; 21, Inn; 22, Despair; 24, Attire; 25, Nickel; 27, Moose.

No. 100

ACROSS. – 1, Paradise lost; 9, Rotunda; 10, Crumble; 11, Knob; 12, Piper; 13, Lamp; 16, Nest-egg; 17, Smother; 18, Rebuffs; 21, Stand on; 23, Mint; 24, Merry; 25, Isis; 28, Shekels; 29, Ill will; 30, Autumn leaves.

DOWN. – 1, Piteous; 2, Rink; 3, Dealing; 4, Suckers; 5, Lout; 6, Sabbath; 7, Broken promise; 8, Pepper and salt; 14, Leafy; 15, Coral; 19, Bandeau; 20, Stetson; 21, Service; 22, Dismiss; 26, Peru; 27, Slav.